"This isn't just another book–with purpose and passion. If yo turner, this is it."

—~~~tor Brian Jones
Author of SeniorPastorCentral.com

"My +20 years in the business world and 10 years in vocational ministry have taught me the value of practical resources for employees. This book is such a resource! Every assistant pastor, regardless of your role in the local church, will benefit from the wisdom shared here."

—**Christopher Sanchez, PhD**
The Southern Baptist Theological Seminary

"*The Art of the Assistant* addresses a neglected topic. There are plenty of books on preaching and leading and caring, but I can't think of any that are exclusively focused on the role of an assistant pastor. Treg covers all the essential aspects of the role with biblical insight and personal experience. He offers wisdom that provides both perspective and practical help, answering the why questions as well as the how. And Treg doesn't shy away from the difficult topics like dealing with criticism, when and how to transition, and even how to work with a poor leader. I would recommend *The Art of the Assistant* for any assistant pastor of any kind, whether you're new to the role or have done it for years."

—**Dan Larison**
Assistant Pastor, Parkside Church

"Treg Spicer has given every God-called assistant pastor a great gift and labor of love in this book. In God's economy, there is no hierarchy of value for His servants—all are vital in the work of the gospel. To every assistant pastor, this book will equip and encourage you to fulfill your calling with Christ-centered devotion and biblical passion. The wisdom in these pages will strengthen you in the journey of serving on a pastoral team!"

—**Cary Schmidt, MMin, DMin**
Senior Pastor, Emmanuel Baptist Church, Connecticut
Author of more than a dozen books and
Host of *Leading in the Gospel* podcast.

Ministering from the MIDDLE

The Art of Becoming a Great Assistant Pastor

TREG SPICER

LUCIDBOOKS

Ministering from the Middle: The Art of Becoming a Great Assistant Pastor
Copyright © 2024 by Treg Spicer
Published by Lucid Books
www.LucidBooks.com

All rights reserved. No part of this publication may be reproduced, stored in a retrieval system, or transmitted in any form by any means, electronic, mechanical, photocopy, recording, or otherwise, without the prior permission of the publisher, except as provided for by US copyright law.

Unless otherwise indicated, Scripture quotations are taken from the King James Version (KJV): King James Version, public domain.

eISBN: 978-1-63296-747-3
ISBN: 978-1-63296-746-6

Special Sales: Most Lucid Books titles are available in special quantity discounts. Custom imprinting or excerpting can also be done.

I dedicate this book to God as a kind of firstfruits offering. I do so, giving complete ownership to Him and trusting in His blessing for the labor that went into this book and upon those who read it (Jer. 30:2).

Table of Contents

Introduction	1
The Art of Communication	9
Art of Physical and Spiritual Well-Being	25
Art of Serving in Your Youth	37
Art of Ministry Transition	49
Art of Dealing with Criticism	63
Art of Discipleship	77
Art of Preaching	91
Art of Purity	103
Art of Suffering	117
Art of Knowing What's Next	131
Art of Dodging Spears	143
Art of Poverty	153
Conclusion	159

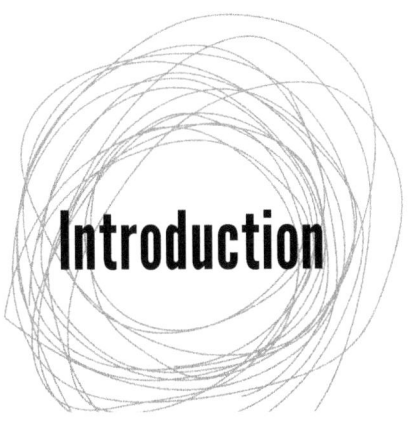

Introduction

Thank you. Thank you for fulfilling your calling as an assistant pastor. Thank you for your desire to serve Jesus and His church. Thank you for the time, energy, and effort you have given to the ministry so it can continue to succeed the way it has. Thank you for the countless hours you have worked behind the scenes with little recognition or applause. Thank you for going the extra mile for guests and visitors to ensure they have a wonderful time at church. Thank you for the sacrifices you have made in service. Thank you for reading this book.

I understand that we are all different in ministry. Your experiences will be different than mine. We are much like fingerprints—we look the same, but we are unique. Pastors and assistant pastors have unique roles, job descriptions, and responsibilities. Every church is different. Cultures and people we serve are different.

Some pastors and assistant pastors are jacks of all trades and masters of none. Some assistants answer only to the pastor and serve the pastor directly, while others tend to assist every person on staff. Some assistant pastors have major responsibilities such as overseeing missions, a Christian school, or small groups. Regardless, your role as an assistant is important to the body of Christ.

Many of you know this is your calling, and you have no desire to do anything else. I have talked to and interviewed many assistants. I love their insight and self-awareness of their gifts and abilities and how they can best be used to serve.

Some of you reading this book are in the same place I was for 16 years. I served as an assistant pastor in three states under three pastors. I enjoyed every one of those days, but I knew in my heart I wanted to be a senior pastor. It was not because it seemed like the logical next move or step but because it was a calling and a desire I developed early in childhood.

I had a list of desires as a child, and many of my memories were centered on those coming to fruition. Much of my childhood is a blur, but the few things I do remember seem to be tied to my being able to accomplish certain things—attending certain sporting events, hitting my first home run, or having the opportunity to lead in some way.

There is one memory I will never forget. Thankfully, phones were still connected to the wall in those days, and there was no easy way to make a video recording. Memories are and will be sufficient. I was in the sixth grade, and I really wanted the lead role in our elementary Christmas play. I auditioned, and sure enough, I got it. I was the lucky student to play Santa in the play called *Santa Goes Hip*. I didn't necessarily want to be Santa; I just wanted to be the lead. That was the beginning of many plays and several lead roles over my junior high school and high school career.

Introduction

Looking back, I realize it wasn't because I was a drama kid; I just wanted to lead in every way I could. I wanted to be president of my classes and fight for the position of team captain in every sport. I wanted to be calling the shots. I wanted to take the credit or blame. As a junior high student, I prayed regularly that God would give me the ability to be the type of upperclassman one day the younger students would look up to. I wanted to lead when I got older. Was that because I liked the notoriety and power? Some might think so. I believe it is just in my DNA to lead.

When I studied for the ministry, I knew there were certain things I did not want to do. I did not want to be a youth pastor or even an assistant pastor. When the college had youth seminars, I skipped them. When pastors called me because they wanted me to be their assistant pastor, I declined their offers. I wanted to be not just a pastor but the senior pastor—the lead pastor.

But God makes it clear that His thoughts are not my thoughts, nor are my ways His ways. My goal of graduating and becoming a lead pastor did not transpire as I had wished or imagined. I was offered a position as an associate pastor with the promise of taking the lead pastor role within five years of my hiring. This was a fantastic opportunity to learn and grow, so I accepted the position. Eleven years later, it was evident that my desire to lead that church would never be a reality, so I began to pray for what was next.

God led me to another ministry where again my desire to be the lead pastor did not happen. Once again, I was an assistant. Despite my desires, I knew this was the Lord's leading, so I followed His direction. It was there that I received the call to

Faith Baptist Church in Morgantown, West Virginia. I would again be an assistant for two years before I was voted in as the second pastor in the church's 49-year history. Finally, in May 2016, God gave me the desire of my heart. God had taught me invaluable lessons as an assistant pastor for 16 years before I transitioned into a well-established ministry.

If you are reading this and thinking, "Yes, that is exactly where I am," then be patient. God does not work on our schedules. Delight yourself in Him and in your current position, and He will give you the desires of your heart (Ps. 37:4).

I hope you will find encouragement and help through the stories I will share. Assistant pastors all over the world have experienced these same stories, and I trust that many of them will resonate with you.

God has led me to write this book for people like Zach who has much potential for the Kingdom of God. Zach is incredibly intelligent, but he is lacking ministerial experience. He landed at Faith through a friend's recommendation. It seemed like a perfect fit for all those involved, and it was.

As Zach was growing up, his pastor had genuinely desired to pour into him and develop him as a young leader. It did not take long for his pastor to see there was not much he could teach this young man. Zach was brilliant, and in many ways, he seemed to have a better handle on Scripture than the pastor did. As a result, the pastor has greatly leaned on Zach for help and direction. The problem is that Zach still feels like he is a novice and needs mentorship. Zach, please let this book be your mentor and guide, and give you what you need to succeed as an assistant pastor.

Introduction

I am writing this book for the assistants at Park Place, a fantastic ministry with many facets and staffing to fulfill its various ministries. Park Place has grown tremendously over the past several years. This growth has been a real challenge for the pastor and the staff to keep up with. The pastor leans heavily on his administrative pastor, but even he finds himself overwhelmed with the pace of growth and the needs associated with that growth. Over the years, Park Place has added several staff members to help with their current needs. They strategically bring on staff as a means to develop the next generation of leaders and pastors. Park Place has done a great job keeping up with its staff during staff meetings and annual retreats, but it knows that what is missing is the assistants' individual development and discipleship. Park Place, I hope this book serves as a study guide for your assistants and proves to be a valuable resource to the leaders and elders who desire to invest in the staff God has given you.

I am also writing this book for Daniel who has taken the offer to be an assistant pastor at his home church, despite being advised otherwise. The average assistant only makes it two years at Shenandoah. Daniel feels that his relationship with the pastor and those in his church will bring about a different experience for him. Daniel is doing well at Shenandoah, but it has more to do with his being home than being in an ideal position.

The pastor is not a bad guy, and he is not difficult to work with, but he is finding that what others have said is true. The pastor is difficult to get to know. He seems very short with Daniel, avoids deep and theological conversations, and doesn't give feedback or advice. It is not a character flaw in the pastor but just a defense he has put up over the years. After investing time and energy in his first few assistants just to have them leave, he has unconsciously guarded himself against being hurt or disappointed by every hire after that. Daniel, I pray this book will be a tool and conduit you can use to help bridge the gap that seems to be between you and your pastor.

I am writing this book for Pastor Rafael who has seemingly struck out with the last few pastors he has hired. They seemed lazy, opinionated, and unwilling to learn. Rafael tried to train and teach them how his pastor did for him 30 years ago, but they never seem interested. Dispensationalism, separation, and textual issues are still relevant today, but Rafael's assistants have shown little desire to learn those things. Rafael understands there is a significant age difference between him and these young men. He understands it could be contributing to the frustration he and his assistants seem to have. Rafael, I hope this book proves to be a relevant and up-to-date resource for you to use with your assistants.

I am writing this book for the wives of assistant pastors. I have seen the hurt and frustration that pastors' wives go through when their husbands are frustrated and looking for more. I have witnessed the tears and anxiety when there seems to be nowhere for these wives to turn and nowhere to run. When they do find help, it is rarely enough. In many ways, they don't understand why their husbands are acting the way they are. They don't know how to encourage them, and the only thing they know to do is support them as they begin to look for a better opportunity. I trust this book will help their husbands find meaning and purpose in their calling. I hope it

INTRODUCTION

brings stability to their homes and marriages. I hope this book will allow their wives to say, "My husband is not the same after reading this."

I am writing this to the assistant pastors who feel alone in their current roles, to the ones who feel like they have been thrown into their current position without guidance or direction. You are talented and gifted, but due to that, your pastor feels you will figure things out on your own. He had little training and has done just fine, and he knows you will be no different.

This charge I commit to you, son Timothy, according to the prophecies previously made concerning you, that by them you may wage the good warfare, These words I entrust to you, assistant pastors, according to what I have learned, known, and been assured of, so that as you are inspired and aided by your pastors, you may fight the good fight of the faith in your current calling and ministry.

The Art of Communication

Jimmy was invited to a conference out of town, and the invitation could not have come soon enough. At that point, he would have accepted an invitation to just about anywhere. Tensions were brewing. The pastor, who was respected and loved, had recently shown stark signs of aging, forgetting things, losing his place while preaching, and going off on crazy tangents. Unfortunately, Jimmy (the young assistant) was fielding all the concerns and complaints. People seemed to assume he had some pull or could do something about it, but it was just the opposite. Jimmy's hands were tied. He dared not say anything. This was God's anointed. Even David didn't raise his hand against King Saul when he had the chance.

Jimmy also was not oblivious to the atmosphere around him. The pastor might not have known exactly what was going on behind the scenes, but he knew Jimmy was winning the people's hearts. Jimmy could sense the tension between him and the pastor. This tension was not necessarily his fault; it was just the evident contrast between their styles and personalities. Things were bad, and there were no signs of them getting better.

This conference could not have come at a better time. Jimmy knew that a few very unhappy people were about to approach the pastor regarding his condition. They were also going to petition that he step down and hand things over to Jimmy. There was no telling how this meeting would go, but Jimmy was glad he was nowhere nearby when it happened.

But 500 miles and important meetings didn't keep Jimmy's phone from ringing that night. "The meeting did not go well" were the first words Jimmy heard. Immediately, a sick feeling hit his stomach. He wasn't sure if he would be able to finish the conversation before going to the restroom to throw up. "Pastor said there was nothing wrong with him or his health," Allan said. "He said he feels better now than he has in years. He told us he had no idea where these accusations originated, and he was going to look into it. He also said this needed to stop immediately."

Jimmy arrived home a few days later. He knew things would be bad. He just didn't know how bad. The tension between him and the pastor was so thick you could cut it with a knife. Communication was sparse between them, to say the least. Jimmy was not surprised. He knew there was no way the pastor would believe his members would dare think such things about him. The pastor would surely believe they had to be driven by another source—Jimmy.

Writing this as a senior pastor myself, I can assure you that at times we are straight-up jerks when it comes to communicating with our associates. I know of one assistant who regularly received a nonverbal communication from his secretary on whether he should walk into the pastor's office or not. She would smile if the mood was good and very slightly shake her head if he needed to stay away.

Some pastors are grumps, but some are just very focused individuals. Stopping all forward momentum in a pastor's studies to talk about Papa Johns or Pizza Hut for the upcoming youth rally can cause more issues in his brain than you might think (and everyone knows the answer is Papa Johns).

Do not avoid the pastor at all costs, even though it might be tempting at times, but strategize and plan the best ways for you to communicate with your senior pastor. It is not always easy, but you must figure out when and if you are bothering him. When is the right time for you to walk into his office? How much is too much? How should you go into a meeting if you suspect there might be a confrontation? How do you confront the pastor over a sin issue? When is it proper to send a text? Should you call? Is it wrong to email him? In this chapter, we will address all these issues and more. Picking the right method of communication is crucial to convey your message properly.

Before we get started, allow me to say this. No matter what method you choose, always keep the pastor informed about what is going on. I can tell you that he doesn't like to be surprised. Don't make him call you to ask where you are or what is happening. You told him about your vacation at least a year ago, but he doesn't remember. Reminders are essential. Don't cancel a youth outing without his knowing first. Just stay in communication. It takes a few seconds to send a text that could prevent hours of frustration.

Jimmy is not the one to be blamed for any of this. He is young and in need of mentoring and maturing. Yet there are some things he could have done to help prevent the storms instead of only preparing for them. If at all possible, Jimmy needed to do everything in his power to keep all communication lines open with his pastor. Sending him a text and saying, "I've heard you have a meeting coming up, and I have no idea what is going to be discussed, but I'm praying," would have gone a long way. Jimmy needed to go above and beyond, never giving him cause for suspicion. The pastor should have had total confidence that Jimmy was not conspiring or contemplating any hostile takeover. Communication is essential for a proper working relationship with all staff. Unfortunately, communication is one of a team's most complicated and frustrating hurdles.

Methods of Communication
Texting

1. Never discuss important matters in a text message. Sam was preaching a revival in a rural community. Upon arriving, he was told he would be eating out with the pastoral staff, but the assistant pastor of that church had no idea where. The assistant had texted the church's pastor several times that afternoon but had received no response. Sam and the assistant sat there in limbo, not knowing where to go. Sam was getting nervous because there was just over an hour before he had to speak. Finally, the pastor called and gave his assistant the name of the place to meet. When Sam and the assistant pulled in, a sign that hung on the door said "Closed." Come to find out, it was always closed on Mondays. Who knew? Obviously, no one on the pastoral staff knew. This wouldn't be a problem in most towns, but considering there were only two restaurants in town, it was. They rushed to the

other end of town, had a quick bite to eat, and returned to church just in time for the service to begin.

All those details should have been taken care of prior to Sam's arrival. Often in staff meetings, discussions about the major events come up, but don't forget the details. Don't assume the pastor has it all figured out. Take time to discuss the details with him.

2. For casual conversations, sending a funny GIF or commenting about the football game over a text is appropriate. Asking to take a mission trip to Africa isn't. It is okay to text now and then, but be respectful of the pastor's time, even if he texts more than you do. Always be sure to respond to his texts immediately.

3. Never text when you are frustrated or mad. I was responsible for running the annual Christian school fundraiser. This year, I wanted to do something different. I decided to give every student a free T-shirt to generate interest and motivate them to participate in the fundraiser. The shirts cost around $5 each, and that cost was covered by corporate sponsorships whose names were clearly printed on the back of the shirts. The senior pastor did not like the idea. I was at home with my family, enjoying Christmas Eve together, when I received a text that said, "I cannot believe you spent almost $300 on T-shirts for the fundraiser. This was a waste of money. One day when you become a pastor, you will ruin your church because of your careless use of money. You need to stop this kind of spending."

How do you respond to that? Did I mention this was sent on December 24? I responded, "I don't feel texting about this on Christmas Eve is the right approach. When we return to work on Monday, I will gladly explain why I did what I did and where the money came from to pay for them." It never came up again.

Emails

There are certain conversations you will want a record of. I highly encourage emails in situations like this. That would be appropriate when dealing with topics such as finances or missions. None of us want our inboxes junked up, but when it comes to important details, you should always put it in an email.

Sam and the church would have avoided frustration if the plans had all been made through emails. After a face-to-face meeting, someone on staff should have put Sam's travel arrangements into an email. It then should have been sent not only to Sam but to all the staff members who would have been involved in his arrival. Email your plans for upcoming events and ask for your pastor's or pastors' input. Email your calendar for the upcoming year. Email your expense reports to the appropriate people on time each year and early, if possible.

Before sending a personal email that will cause a shock-and-awe effect, sleep on it. I can remember writing two such emails in the past 20 years. One of them I wish I'd never sent, and one of them I'm glad I never sent. I wrote the first email after a young family informed us they were leaving the church. I was lying in bed that night and couldn't sleep after hearing this news, so I typed an email of frustration and unfortunately hit send instead of sleeping on it. The email was printed and handed out to the other pastors, the deacons, and several members. It was a mess. Had I sent the other email, I possibly would not be writing this book from my desk in Morgantown. I slept on it, prayed over it, and saved it. Now it serves as a constant reminder to sleep before sending. Typing emails out of frustration is a great thing. It is a way to journal your thoughts, which can be very helpful and therapeutic. But just don't send the email until you have had time to pray about it and sleep over it (the same applies to texting).

A Written Letter

Like an email, be very careful when you send a written letter. Letters are similar to emails. Everything you write could be interpreted the wrong way, and you can't control who sees your letter or how public it may become. Even when a written letter is meant to be constructive, it can have a negative connotation. Letters tend to get circulated. Letters often get twisted and taken out of context. Understand that when you send a letter, it might be read by the pastor's wife, his family, the board, and everyone on Facebook. Choose your words carefully.

Confrontational letters. I have written a few confrontational letters in the past. They were very carefully worded and direct. I had a point to make, and I made it. I wrote one letter while sitting on the front row of the auditorium. I wanted to be in the most "spiritual place" I could be while writing this letter to confront a local pastor whose sin was brought to my attention.

Anonymous letters. I hate anonymous letters. I have debated over and over whether it is even worth my time to read them. If a person doesn't have the guts to put their name on the letter, why should I take the time to read it? Pastor Dwight L. Moody found a note on the pulpit one Sunday when he arrived. The note simply read, "FOOL." Moody stepped up to the pulpit and said, "I have received many anonymous letters in my time, but this is the first time I have ever received a letter that had nothing on it other than the person's signature." To think that even Moody received anonymous letters is comforting. Even though these letters are usually full of slander and insults, there is sometimes a silver lining of truth that you can take into consideration.

My pastor received an anonymous letter, and it was all about me. The majority of the letter was crazy, but I did consider one point. During a graduation ceremony at our Christian school, I was seated behind the lectern where the graduation speaker addressed the students. One position I took while listening to the speech was with both feet on the ground and my arms crossed. The letter's author informed the pastor that I was extremely jealous of the speaker and had expressed it with my body language that night. This simply wasn't true. But I'm now much more aware of how I sit in public—as we all should be. In his book *Amplify Your Influence*, René Rodriguez says, "We need to ask ourselves why we make a certain movement and what causes those micro-expressions. Then, make the internal changes necessary to eliminate."

If you read the letter, glean some truth from it and throw it away. My pastor took the above-mentioned letter and kept it in a file in his briefcase. He carried it with him mentally and literally everywhere he went. Please don't give Mr. or Mrs. Anonymous that much credit.

Signing letters. Never sign a letter you are not comfortable with. My former pastor once wrote a letter informing an employee of their termination. He called me into his office to sign the letter after it was written. I did not feel the letter was done correctly. It contained assumptions and made accusations that were not fair to the employee. I believed it would cause a major stink, but I signed it anyway. As I write this today, I still regret my decision. Later that week, the letter went to Facebook, and I was tagged in it. It was bad. I am now very careful, as you should be, before putting a signature on any letter, campaign, or agenda.

Phone calls. Don't hesitate to call your pastor. If you have a question that needs an immediate answer or want to let him know something of importance, call. Respect his day off and study times if at all possible. Only call him if you don't see a face-to-face conversation happening in the immediate future. I receive very few calls from my staff, but when I do, I answer them as soon as possible.

Face-to-face. Ask questions. Take opportunities to have one-on-ones with your pastor. Those times can prove to be very valuable and rewarding. If you don't have a scheduled time to meet with him, ask if you can have one. Even if it is every other week or once a month, you can learn a lot from him. You might think, "Treg, you don't know my pastor." True. But go into the meeting with a list of questions you can ask to help you in the future.

My friend, Cary Schmit, recommends approaching this with these words: "I know your time is valuable, and I promise not to waste it. I will take everything you share with me and use it to further Christ's Kingdom."

Here are a few questions you can take with you.
1. How did you know God wanted you to take the pastorate at this church?
2. What are some things you would tell a 25-year-old you?
3. What commentary did you use to get the information you did on that verse on Sunday?
4. What is your take on these topics, and why?
   - divorce and remarriage
   - social drinking
   - fasting
   - dating
   - tithing
   - church discipline
   - degrees of separation
   - deacons' authority
   - debt
   - social media
5. What books have made the most significant impact on your life?
6. What have been the most enormous hurdles you have had to jump in ministry?
7. What do you struggle with the most?

Always have a notebook and pen with you, and be ready to write, especially if your pastor is wise with much to offer. A teachable spirit is essential for a man in ministry. You want to be constantly learning. Asking questions guarantees you will be availing yourself of opportunities for knowledge on a regular basis.

I would also take advantage of guest speakers when they come. Ask the pastor if you can take the speaker to lunch. Talk to the speaker ahead of time about your plan, and then go in with questions blazing. This is the way to grow in wisdom and experience beyond your years.

When confrontation comes. It can be a scary thing when you are called into the boss's office. We will deal more with confrontation later, but how do you communicate properly when you're called into the office?

Martha, the church secretary, did not trust any decision unless the pastor made it. She had been with Pastor Thompson for over 30 years. Every time one of the assistants did something she didn't like, Pastor Thompson would soon hear about it.

On this particular day, the staff knew it was coming. They had done something completely out of the norm, and they could tell that Martha didn't like it. As soon as the pastor returned to the office, they all heard forceful whispering. The text messages started to fly among the staff. They were all guessing who would take the blame for this one. When the whispers stopped, footsteps could be heard marching toward the youth pastor's office. A sigh of relief went over the other staff members as they listened intently through their doors. It was much like siblings waiting to see exactly what kind of punishment their siblings were about to receive. Before the pastor even entered his subordinate's office, the lecturing and berating began. To everyone's surprise, the youth pastor interrupted and said, "Pastor, you don't know the whole story. If you would like to sit down and talk about this like men, I would love to fill you in on the details you are missing."

The pastor said, "No, it doesn't matter anyway." He walked out, and it never came up again. A few minutes later, applause emojis from the other staff members flooded the youth pastor's phone.

Confrontation stinks. Very few look forward to conversing about a sensitive or controversial subject. When you are called into a situation like this, there are a few things I encourage you to remember.

1. Remember to hand this over to God prayerfully.
2. Remember that we wrestle not against flesh and blood. The pastor is not your enemy. Don't go into a meeting with guns blazing at anyone except the devil.
3. Remember to follow up with questions, not accusations. Peter Scazzero in his book *The Emotionally Healthy Leader* suggests opening with the line, "I'm puzzled on why you did this." You could start with, "Pastor, I'm puzzled about why you decided to cut my youth budget. Can you explain the reason behind this to me, please?"
4. Remember to be objective. Do not make it personal. It might be, but don't allow it to be at that moment. Try seeing it from both sides.
5. Remember that playing the conversation over and over again in your head accomplishes nothing. Trying to figure out what is going to be said and how you will respond is a futile exercise that will produce excess stress and anxiety. You can role-play with a trusted advisor or friend if you are truly nervous about the conversation. Have them play the role of the pastor and instruct

them on how you feel he might respond. Have them talk through different scenarios, which will give you confidence before the meeting.

Regardless of how or why you were approached, it is essential to remember the words of Solomon. "A soft answer turneth away wrath" (Prov. 15:1).

When confrontation needs to be delivered. Now, let's flip the script. What are the steps you should take if you are the one calling staff members into your office?

1. Prepare. Before you have a difficult conversation, take some time to prepare yourself mentally, emotionally, and prayerfully. Write down your goals and intentions for the conversation. Stay on task, and don't get sidetracked.
2. Choose a time and place where you and the other person can speak openly and without interruptions. Ensure the setting is private and comfortable and allow enough time for the conversation to unfold. Coffee shops or restaurants can be appropriate for less threatening conversations.

Here's an example, not of confrontation but of the right time and place. I had heard that my youth pastor wanted to approach me about a raise. I was also told he was nervous about it. When he asked me for a meeting, I asked, "What is it about?" He gulped and told me. I said, "Sure, how about we do that at Penn Station Subs? I'll drive and buy." Immediately, it took the pressure off of him and created a non-threatening environment.

3. Start the meeting with a positive tone. Express your appreciation for the other person and their willingness to talk with you. Use "I" statements to express your thoughts and feelings and avoid blaming or accusing.
4. Clearly state the problem or issue you want to discuss. Be specific and avoid generalizations.
5. Listen actively and carefully to the other person's perspective without interrupting or judging. Try to understand where they are coming from and ask open-ended questions to clarify their points of view.
6. Brainstorm possible solutions together and explore all options. Be open to compromise and find common ground. Focus on finding a solution that works for both of you.
7. Follow up by summarizing the conversation and any agreements you reached. Make sure you both have a clear understanding of what you both discussed and decided. Follow up with any action steps or further communication that may be necessary.

None of us is perfect, and if we are not careful, these heated conversations could lead to rash decisions or saying things we regret for years to come. There are going to be battles with our words. When you find yourself in the ring, be wise. Take the punch on the chin if needed, know when to duck, and be very careful with your counterpunches.

TIME TO REFLECT

1. Think back on a conversation with a boss or pastor. How could you have handled it differently? Why?
2. Look through your text history with your pastor. Are there text messages that should have been personal conversations or emails? If so, what can you do to recognize that before hitting "send" in the future?
3. If conversation is an ongoing issue, find resources to help you with your words. I would recommend the following books:

War of Words: Getting to the Heart of Your Communication Struggles, by Paul David Tripp

The Emotionally Healthy Leader, by Pete Scazzero

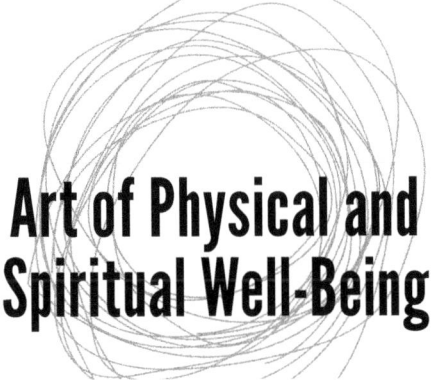

Art of Physical and Spiritual Well-Being

Physical Well-Being

I remember my very first day working as a "real" pastor. I was 22 years old and had just finished my undergraduate studies. I was hired by the church that hosted the Christian school I attended from junior high through my senior year in high school. I was so excited to finally put into practice what I had studied so long to do. I had taught Sunday school and had been preaching on and off since I was 16, but this was the first time I was actually getting paid to do it. After church Sunday morning I was excited to talk with the pastor and get my orders for the first day in the office.

Let's just say it was not what I expected. The pastor told me to meet him the next day at the tennis court at 9:00 a.m. I wasn't sure if we were going to be witnessing to people in the park or what. He then said, "And make sure you have your racquet with you." It was an amazing morning, to say the least. It was a first day of work—a day I have never forgotten. It was most memorable. We played tennis all morning. The two things I remember most were getting beat by a 65-year-old pastor who drank coffee between sets, even though it was 90 degrees outside with 90 percent humidity.

What was the point of that? Is there some secret about tennis that helps develop shepherds? No. Was the pastor secretly watching my temperament to see if I would throw my racquet against the fence when I missed a shot? No. It was simply a pastor who valued the discipline of hard work and knew the overall importance of exercise both mentally and physically.

He also push-mowed his lawn every week. It was a well-treated and manicured lawn that he made sure was always 4 inches high. He could have easily justified a riding lawn mower or even paid someone to mow it, but he always said he did it because he enjoyed the exercise and working up a sweat.

The Apostle Paul makes it clear that bodily exercise profits for a little time, but he never argues that it doesn't profit. Over the years, I have realized that my first day on the job was one that taught me more than I ever acknowledged at the time.

Exercise Does as Much if Not More for Us Mentally as Physically

There is a lot of pressure that comes with shepherding the flock. We have sheep coming to us seeking counsel and advice on how to deal with things we might never face personally. I am currently working with a young man whose wife walked out on him (and for good reason). Just a few weeks ago, a man texted me early in the morning (I was at Planet Fitness) and asked if we could meet ASAP. He came into my office broken and anxious. He then proceeded to tell me that the night before they had found out that their daughter, who was in kindergarten, had been sexually abused. For obvious reasons, this had extenuating circumstances that prohibited me from telling anyone about them.

This is our calling, but this is also a great burden we carry with our calling. Mentally, exercise is a must in order for us to be able to deal with such overbearing burdens. You might be thinking, "Treg, that is what video games are for." No. Unlike video games, exercise reduces adrenaline and cortisol. It also stimulates the production of endorphins, the body's natural painkillers and mood elevators. You could say exercise is God's natural anxiety medication. Taking care of our body and mind is a testimony that we truly value the temple God has given us.

My wife continually tells me we need to make sure our church decor and grounds are valued and taken care of. She then makes a comparison of how detailed God was in taking care of the temple. As a good husband and pastor, I always remind her that the temple is no longer a building but our bodies. Despite how comfortable my couch is, I have decided to stop reminding my wife of that when she brings up the temple. How can we preach about the sin of the body when our bodies are a mess?

Our pastoral staff has been accused of being the fittest pastoral staff in West Virginia. That is not my goal or desire, but I do want to honor God in both my spirit and my body. I want younger men to look at me and acknowledge that not all pastors sit behind desks continually. You owe this to your wife, family, congregation, and the next generation. Get up and do something!

Exercise Can Ensure You Are Healthy and Mobile for Long-Term Ministry

All the knowledge and experience you gain in ministry is too valuable to throw away when you are 60 because you lack drive, motivation, and energy. Don't just take care of your body and exercise for the now but for the future 25 years down the road. I am not recommending that we all have biceps like Craig Groeschel, but I am saying that you should have regular exercise as a daily routine in your already busy schedule.

If physical fitness was all that was involved in our overall well-being, we would have it made. That honestly is the easy part. And if that were the case, I would recommend you all become fitness trainers, and all our problems will be solved. As you know, that is not the case.

SPIRITUAL WELL-BEING
Prayer

There are hundreds of books on prayer for a reason. There is no one way to pray. We can pray like Daniel and see results. We can pray 2 Chronicles 7:14 every day at 7:14 a.m. and see results. We can pray the prayer of Jabez . . . well . . . I'll stop there. God does not honor one prayer over another because of the time we pray or if we eat Daniel's diet or Domino's pizza after we pray.

The truth is, much like our physical health, what works for one in prayer is not the answer for all. There is no this-is-the-only-way solution to prayer. There is no secret book or program to buy that will specifically bless you or your family. No pastor or evangelist can give you the secrets of spiritual success so you will never struggle again. The secret formula just does not exist.

So my encouragement to you today is to pray. Read. Spend time with God. There is only one way to know Him (Phil. 3:10), and that is to spend time with Him. As assistant pastors or senior pastors, I think we lack an appreciation and realization of how powerful prayer is and how necessary it is for our current ministry.

There are three reasons why prayer is so essential for assistant pastors.
1. Prayer changes things.
2. Prayer changes you.
3. Prayer moves the hand of God.

Elijah was just like us. His fervent, earnest prayer held off the rain for three and a half years. His prayer changed things in Israel (James 4:17). He prayed, and fire came down from heaven. His prayer changed the hearts of the people. He prayed, and God answered in a still, small voice. His prayer changed his outlook on life.

As assistants, we focus on others and ministry while neglecting the most important thing. We are in hero mode with our capes on, wanting to solve problems, picking up the pieces left behind, and doing all we can to shine. We quickly brag about how many hours we work a week, but I have yet to have an assistant brag about how many hours he prays. Do you think God is looking at how you punch the time clock or stop the clock in the prayer closet? It is not until we realize what we can accomplish for God and ourselves by prayer that we will find breakthroughs in our lives and ministries.

Alright, Treg, you might be saying, if there is no secret recipe or divine design, how do I need to pray? First, allow me to give you some practical advice.

1. *Find a place to pray.* This can often be the most challenging task of all. If you have an office, tell your administrative assistant you are not to be bothered from 8:00 a.m. to 9:00 a.m. If you would rather pray at home, set up a prayer closet. It could be a literal closet, the basement, or the shed out back. Wherever it is, make sure it is secluded and a place where you can be alone with God.

2. *Find a particular time to pray.* Consistency is the key. You'd better believe that every great athlete is committed to consistent workouts and routines. You'd better believe that Tom Brady followed the same diet, workout routine, and drills day in and day out. He is who he is because of commitment and consistency. If you desire to be a GOAT (greatest of all time) for God, you must be consistent and committed to prayer.

   Find a time that works best for you. Mornings are the only time I can find peace and quiet. You might find that nights are the best time to pray. Whatever time you choose, please be consistent. Make an appointment with God at this time every day. Don't miss your appointments with God.

3. *Have a plan to pray.* Again, I can assure you that Brady does not walk into the gym and wonder what he is going to do. He knows exactly what his workout will be before entering the gym. Unfortunately, we go before the Lord without knowing how or what we are praying. We fumble

until we feel like we've prayed for everyone we know and then go on with our day. Instead of fumbling your way through, set up a plan. Here is a sample to get you started.

Monday: Missions
Tuesday: Terrific people in my life (friends)
Wednesday: Witness (pastors local and global)
Thursday: Taken requests (from your Wednesday prayer service if you have one)
Friday: Family (extended, immediate, every day by name)
Saturday: Summit Ridge (my neighborhood)
Sunday: Sermon, the spirit and strength to preach the Scriptures

The Scriptures

The Bible is another key to developing your spiritual well-being. I'm concerned that Bible reading often gets put to the side or becomes more of a subject than a spiritual tool. A few years ago, I asked a pastor what he was doing for devotional time. He said a particular book of the Bible. That was great except it was the series he was preaching through. That can work, but I don't recommend it. It's mixing work with spiritual well-being.

The Scriptures were so important to Paul that his last request to Timothy was to bring the Scriptures to him. Daniel looked for answers about the captivity and found them in the Scriptures. Peter says everything we need for life and godliness is found in the Scriptures. You must make the Bible a regular part of your life.

When asked about Bible reading on a Q&A panel, I heard a well-known pastor jokingly say he was on a two-year reading plan. He said, "I'm just a little slow." Everyone laughed. He never really answered the question. A few years later he was caught in an affair. The affair had been going on for almost eight years. I believe he dodged the question because he was not able to answer it.

Again, there is no single best way or a divinely inspired reading plan. Just make sure you are in God's Word. My recommendation is to read through the Bible. If you have never done that, please do. I would also encourage those of you who enjoy a challenge to read through the Bible in 90 days. YouVersion has a 90-day reading plan. I promise you, it will change your life. Reading that much Scripture and that much of each book in that time will give you a perspective you have never had. If you like to write, I recommend a journaling Bible or a personal journal. I have one for Job and one for John. That allows you to not only read that book of the Bible but also to write down what the passage is saying to you.

Meditation

Meditation is another key aspect of spiritual well-being. We like to use that word and avoid it all at the same time. Meditation is a word I have heard preached since I was a kid. One favorite passage of Scripture that deals with meditation is Joshua 1:8. I often hear the word *meditation* used in sermons and lessons in conjunction with the idea of "chewing the cud." And if you did not have the privilege of growing up in southeastern Ohio like I did, you might not know exactly what I'm referring to. Well, a cow has four chambers in its stomach. Each one can store a considerable amount of food. When the old girl gets hungry, she can burp up that partially digested alfalfa from stomach number three and enjoy it again. There are certain features animals have that I feel humans should also have. The idea here is chewing on what has been partially digested. This is how meditation has been described to me. I am by no means saying that is wrong. But my question is this: Is there more to it? Should there not be any more to it?

Eastern Philosophy vs. Christian Philosophy

Martial arts were a huge part of my life growing up. I remember asking Dad countless times to teach me martial arts. I wanted to learn so badly. He always said, "When you can do a split and touch your nose to the ground, I will teach you." I worked and worked at it until I finally got it. I am sure if you were to film my childhood, it would be the perfect martial arts movie as I tried every day to tear my hamstrings in two to get my nose to the ground. Even though Dad started teaching me, he never let me take classes. He did not want me involved in all that was tied to martial arts, primarily meditation.

According to USA Taekwondo, "Meditation and Taekwondo (all martial arts, for that matter) go hand in hand. Athletes who have worked with us have reported that they feel and perform better when they meditate regularly as part of their training."

They are not talking about chewing the cud. So where do we draw the line? What is the right and wrong here? Early in my ministry, a movement was taking shape, and everyone was reading, writing, and speaking for or against it. It was called the

Emergent Church. This movement brought popularity to yoga and other forms of Eastern mysticism in the religious circles of the day. It singlehandedly destroyed any chance for meditation to be promoted in any conservative church. The effects of this still linger today. But are we missing something by "throwing the baby out with the bath water"?

Eastern meditation. First, we must understand when dealing with the Eastern philosophy of meditation that a basic description of meditation is a supposedly higher or altered state of consciousness. Meditation is practiced to suspend rational thought patterns to clear the mind. So Eastern meditation is the emptying of the mind. Many of you are thinking what I've often thought, that "my teen boys must be in a constant state of meditation."

Christian meditation. Let's talk now about Christian meditation. Is there a place for it? Should it be part of my daily or weekly rhythm? Do I need it in order to be the Christian I need to be? Yes!

In Hebrew, there are two words for our English word *meditate*. Both carry similar ideas, and when used in Scripture, they emphasize an end result. For instance, by meditating on Scripture, the blessed man in Psalm 1 will "bear fruit." Joshua was promised success.

So what is meditation? It is simply the ability to "set our minds on things above" (Col. 3:4). By doing that, we are in tune with what the Scriptures and the Spirit are saying to us. We are putting ourselves in the position to hear the voice of God. I am quick to sing "Before the Throne of God Above," but I am slow or negligent in going there. In a day and age of noise and distraction, we need to be intentional about our meditation.

Practical Applications for Christian Meditation

How do we meditate—the right way? I recommend taking a passage or event in Scripture and putting yourself in it. Meditation is not commentary. It is complementary. It is not just what the passage means but how the passage can change you. If you're unsure how to practice meaningful Christian meditation, try the following two approaches.

Meditate on an event. Take the event of Jesus turning the water into wine in John 2 and read it a few times. Then put yourself at that wedding. Look at the crowd. Enjoy the fellowship of others and Jesus. See Mary walking around making sure all the guests are well taken care of. Then watch the devastation as the word goes out that there is no more wine. Listen to the complaints and the critics. Listen to the bride and the governor of the feast as they are ridiculed. You might even hear complaints that Jesus brought too many guests. Now, watch the Savior do His work. How does that one passage speak to you? Have you ever found yourself in the position of the bride, of Mary, or of one of the guests?

Meditate on Scripture. Let's meditate on Revelation 3 when Jesus says, "Behold, I stand at the door and knock." What does that mean to you? What area of your life does Jesus want access to? When was the last time you opened your life to Him? When is the last time you shared a "meal" with Jesus? When was the last time the two of you had fellowship?

I did everything "right" and still had a heart attack. I had a difficult time processing how I could do so much and yet still be so sick. My diet was clean, and I ran every day. A cardiologist who came to see me made a statement that changed this thought process completely. He said, "It was your running that kept you alive. Your arteries were so large that even though your left ventricle was blocked, your heart was still receiving enough blood to keep going."

I can't promise that doing all of the good things in your routine will keep you from falling any more than drinking smoothies kept me from a heart attack. But by making them a regular practice, I can promise you that you will have the strength to get back up. "For a just [righteous] man falleth seven times, and riseth up again" (Prov. 24:16).

TIME TO REFLECT

1. If you were to grade your spiritual well-being on a scale of 1 to 10, where would you fall?
2. Looking at your current state, how can you make improvements to this number immediately?
3. Create a spot on your calendar today and a location that is marked specifically "Time with God."

Art of Serving in Your Youth

"It is a terrible shame that God has wasted all that energy on youth." I have heard this many times over the years. This is not the case. The Apostle John in his epistles even celebrates this energy by saying, "I write unto you, young men, because ye have overcome the wicked one. . . . I have written unto you, young men, because ye are strong, and the word of God abides in you, and ye have overcome the wicked one" (1 John 2:13–14). John wrote to the young men because they overcame the wicked one. Young men are strong. Young men are ready to fight. Young men are willing to stand against the powers of darkness and anything or anyone on their side. Young men are warriors. A young man ran from Potifer's wife, and an old king called for another man's wife to join him for the evening. Paul tells Timothy to allow no man to despise his youth. Paul did not want Timothy to be timid or allow others to look down on him due to his age. Youth is not a curse. Youth is a blessing.

I would consider myself strong when I was a youth but also equally stupid. If you have ever attended a conference that puts together a panel for Q&A, you know that one question that is asked without fail is this: "If you could tell a younger you anything as you look back, what would it be?" The answer usually has something to do with not worrying about things or not sweating the little things. Love people more. Don't be consumed with what people think.

That sounds admirable coming from a 70-year-old, but as young men, you will be dealing with the little things. Why? Because big things haven't happened yet in your life. Sweating the little things prepares us to face the big things when they come crashing down on us. For me to answer this question requires a chapter, not a paragraph. My goal is for you to be smarter than I was and only half as stupid.

Let me encourage you to use your youth for the glory of God. Use your youth to learn as much as you can. Now is the time! Now is the time to learn, grow, and soak in knowledge. Read as much as you can. Mark up the books you read. I know there is a novelty in having a physical book in hand, but the electronic versions can one day be of much more value. I love being able to go back and with one click find every sentence I highlighted. If I know there is a story I need for an illustration in a certain book, I can quickly enter a keyword and search for it electronically.

Surround yourself with wise men. Listen and learn both the good and the bad from them. Watch sermons from all types of pastors and listen to all types of podcasts. Be open-minded in your learning but closed in your convictions.

I would also encourage you to learn hobbies. Use this time to master that skill you have desired to master. This is the time to get those golf lessons. Take out your camera and learn how to shoot quality photos. Learn how to lay tile or hardwood flooring. Whatever it is, learn it now.

Use Your Youth to Enjoy as Much as You Can

Enjoy life in your youth. Take opportunities to travel, camp, hike, visit friends, and fellowship. Opportunities for these things will not necessarily disappear as you age, but I promise you that the opportunity to do these things will dwindle. With four teenagers, I spend more time in a car driving them to activities and ballgames than I do sleeping.

Enjoy your singleness. If you are not married, use that as a gift God has given you for this time in your life. Take the time you have to invest in others. Volunteer for a variety of outings and events you would not have time for otherwise. This is a great time to help coach a sports team. It is an ideal time to get involved in community events and outings.

Enjoy your spouse. Now is the time to, as Solomon says, rejoice with the wife of your youth (Prov. 5:18). This is not the time to spend hours away from her; it is time to spend hours together and grow together. This is the time to enjoy the love and romance God has given you. Be spontaneous. Be you. Don't act like an old married couple. You will have plenty of time for that when you are my age.

Don't Allow Anyone to Despise Your Youth

Like Paul, I want to exhort you to not allow anyone to despise your youth. Youth can be a threat to the older generation. It is easy for older pastors like me to become paranoid in thinking that everyone will vote my old self out and the new energetic pastor into my position. If you feel you are in a ministry where this is happening and it is evident to others, prayerfully consider moving on. Adam knew this feeling all too well. He was by far the youngest man on staff, by about 50 years. He was brought on to take over the ministry when he was just out of college. The magic number for him was five. He was to take over in five years. That would have put him at age 30. The senior pastor was 68, and his plan was to retire at 73. It seemed like a perfect plan; that is, until it wasn't.

Adam was two years into his verbal agreement of five years. Married and expecting their firstborn, Adam and his wife were in an exciting time of their lives. But Adam was hearing rumors now that the pastor wasn't sure he would retire at age 73. The pastor had told one close friend, who shared it with Adam later, that he was thinking of not retiring until he was 75. Adam didn't know what to do. There was nothing in writing, and he could not force the pastor to do anything. He was the outsider, and if anyone was leaving, it would be him. Adam is not alone. I have received calls from countless assistants who have found themselves being despised in similar situations.

Looking back on my youth, I can see where I was despised at times, but I can assure you I also brought some of that on myself. I shake my head as I look back on the pastor I was. There were mistakes I wish I would have never made, things I wish I would have done, words I should have never spoken, emails I wish I had never sent, and letters I should not have mailed. I despise my youth when thinking about them. At the same time, I can look back and remember things I am glad I did, words I am glad I said, and people I am glad I allowed to mentor and teach me. As they say, failure is not the opposite of success; it's part of success. I have failed many times. I write this next section based on those failures and some wins, and I pray they might keep you from the many mistakes I made in ministry.

What I Wish I Had Done
Education
The greatest regret I have looking back on my ministry is that I did not finish my graduate work when I was young. Walking across the stage at age 45 to receive your master's degree is not ideal. Once our second child was born, there was no way Carrie and I could afford my classes. The church would not help either. I was told, "As long as you know your English Bible, you do not need any further education. I see no need for you to go to those cemeteries anyway."

It might not have been said exactly like that, but it was close. So, 12 credit hours into my graduate degree, I was out. It was something that always hung over my head. I knew it was out of my control, but in the back of my mind, I couldn't help feeling like I had quit. I am thankful to finally have my degree, but I so wish I had completed it before 30, not 50.

Life Insurance
Another regret I have is not getting life insurance. As a young, vibrant, newly married 24-year-old, dying was the last thing on my mind. I had better things to worry about. I did have a policy on the house that it would be paid off in case of my death, but that was it. Little did I know that twice in two years I would come face-to-face with death and not die, only by God's grace. If I had died of either the heart attack or the sepsis from

Crohn's disease, my wife and kids would have been left with nothing. I have seen GoFundMe pages set up for young widows far too often. Death is uncertain, and none of us are promised tomorrow. If you are reading this right now and do not have life insurance, mark this page, pick up the phone, and get it today. A $250,000 term life policy won't cost you much, and it's better than nothing. You owe your wife and kids that security.

Retirement

Looking back, I also wish I would have started putting money into a retirement account. I will never be able to go back and make up for lost time on this one. There is no "one day when I am 45." Interest doesn't backtrack. Now is the time to start putting a little away here and there in a Roth IRA. If you want to play the stock market, go ahead, but don't call me for advice. The Roth IRA needs to be above and beyond any stock market investments. A few hundred here and $25 there will add up quickly. They say the way to real wealth is "one house and one spouse." In ministry, the spouse thing we've got, but the house is not always easy. I am in my 11th house.

Retirement is not quitting. It is a way to serve and minister to others without the pressure of a paycheck. I can give my time and resources for ministry and missions without being held back. By putting money away for retirement, you are setting yourself up for a stress-free older life of service.

Journal

I so wish I had kept a consistent journal. I have journaled since college, but not consistently. If I had journaled my experiences over the years as an assistant, I would have ended up with a two-volume set. I would love to go back and see my emotional state as a 26-year-old or get a glimpse of things to see if they were as bad or as good as I remember. One entry in my journal I am thankful I have is the one I wrote three days before my heart attack. I wrote, "Haven't felt like running in days. I am not sure what my problem is." I know now what it was.

Many benefits come from journaling. I will not take the time to go through all those now, but let me encourage you to write in a journal. I love taking my fountain pen every morning and writing about (1) the things of the previous day, (2) three reasons I am thankful for something or someone, and (3) what my life will look like either tomorrow or five years from now. It seems odd or maybe even pointless in the moment, but looking back, this practice has made a major impact on my life and mental health.

Podcast

I wish I had continued with my podcast. In 2011, I put out my first podcast—Podbean—which I still use. I thought it was the coolest thing in the world. I enjoyed it, but I didn't see the point after a few episodes. I can only imagine where it would have gone if I had stayed with it. I might have been writing this from my private island.

What I Am Glad I Did
Family

I am glad my wife and I had children when we did. Four kids in five years was quite the adventure. That was not our plan. I can still remember the day Carrie called and told me she was pregnant when our second child was only six months old. Right then, I knew this child was either going to be a fantastic servant of God or the anti-Christ because he wasn't supposed to be here. Cade, if you are reading this right now, I think you are amazing, and God knew exactly what he was doing. Love ya, man.

Carrie and I will be considered relatively young when we are empty nesters. By the time I turn 50, all four of my children will have graduated from high school. We have had some long, trying days, and that is why the password for our home Wi-Fi network is "4 and no more." The cost of having four kids all close in age is a killer when you consider sports, shoes, clothes, camp, music lessons, and vehicle insurance. And if you have never tried packing up six bikes or kayaks and going somewhere, you are missing out.

Having four teenagers in the house is fantastic. This is by far my favorite stage. Seeing them go from kids to adults and watching God work through them is fantastic. I would not have changed anything—and I would not have had any more.

Travel

I am also thankful I took the majority of my mission trips when I was in my 20s and 30s. I remember asking a pastor to consider going with me to India. He said there was no way he could go. He said he was busier in ministry than he had ever been, and with his kids being teens and in sports, there was just no way he could get away. He then told me he was glad I was going at my age. He said now is the time to go on these trips. I was a little disappointed with him and knew he was wrong. How could now be the time? I had four little ones, and life was crazy. It surely had to be easier to go at his stage of life. After all, teens are self-sufficient and require little from their mom in their dad's absence. Now I am at the age he was when he told me this. I can testify that he was right. Go now! This is the time to go to the east and west, young man. When I left for college, I had only been outside Ohio once. By the time I turned 38, I had been to India twice, the Philippines, Maui, South Africa, and the Caribbean. Those memories and experiences greatly influenced me, allowing me to become who I am today.

Finances

I am also glad that on an early summer day in 2005, I heard a financial advisor speaking on our Christian radio station. He said things that made perfect sense and brought me to great conviction. After hearing that 30-minute sermon, I went to the library and checked out his book. We were camping at the time, so I read the book at the campground and almost put a for sale sign on the camper before we left. We became devoted to getting out of debt. I sold my car and bought an old Oldsmobile for $100. No, the dollar was not worth more back then. When it rained, I got wet. When a snowplow pushed snow over my car, the snow filled the car. It had more bubbles in the window tint than my kids had in their bubble baths. We didn't stick to the no-debt philosophy our whole lives, but we did live by many of the principles and still do.

Mentors

Surrounding myself with older men was something I valued in my early 20s. I can still remember conversations, both casual and professional, while sitting at a table alongside pastors and administrators during local and multi-state meetings. I picked up guest speakers at the airport and asked them questions as we traveled back to their lodging. I enjoyed fellowship with missionaries as they sat around our table getting to know us, and us them. All of these were relationships I began over 20 years ago, and many of them I still value as friends today. In those days, I had nothing to offer but everything to learn, and I did.

Preaching

Chapels, nursing homes, boys' homes—it didn't matter where—I preached every chance I could. It is not always the largest crowds or amazing venues that develop you into an excellent communicator. I found that being able to preach while a resident in a nursing home starts yelling or wheeling their chair up to the pulpit is the best practice. I am thankful for the 16 years I served as an assistant. God taught me so much in those 16 years that I can now write about in this book. God gave me incredible experiences in my first ministry that honed and developed my pastoral ministry and preaching skills. I was the third man on staff in an area where most churches only had one. That allowed me to become the de facto assistant pastor in multiple churches. I preached so often in neighboring churches that some joked that I was on their payroll. Preaching for these men allowed me to see how other churches operated and allowed me to develop as a speaker.

TIME TO REFLECT

1. What can you change today in order to avoid making the same mistakes I made?
2. Find some companies you can trust and set up a life insurance policy.
3. If you have questions, feel free to reach out. My email is treg@faithwv.org.

Art of Ministry Transition

Juan had finally landed the perfect pastoral position. Not only was he serving under a godly pastor, but he was also under the mentorship of some very mature men in ministry. He knew this would be where he could grow and develop, not only as a pastor but as a person. He also could not have had a more perfect job description. It was everything he had always desired to do and more. It wasn't a head pastor position, but that was okay. That would happen in God's timing. He still had a lot to learn.

After a year, things were great. Juan had no regrets and was thriving in the ministry God had called him to. It was early spring, and Juan was attending a conference on a college campus nearby. While there, he ran into James, a man he knew from a ministry about four hours from where Juan was serving. The ministry was significantly more extensive and very healthy. Juan was shocked when James told him his pastor was leaving. He was even more shocked when James told him the pulpit committee brought his name up as a possible candidate for the position. Juan was in a quandary. He loved his position and church, not to mention he had only been there a year, but he knew he had always wanted to be a senior pastor.

As I write these words, a feeling of gut-wrenching sickness comes over me. Leaving our ministries over the years has been one of the hardest things we have ever had to do. It is something like death. These are people you love. You are leaving people you have poured your life into. Not only that, but your people for the most part will not understand. "Why would he leave us? Is that church better than ours? Just because they are bigger doesn't make them any more special. I don't know why he would leave, especially when you look at all the things we have done for him."

Several years after leaving one ministry, I received a message from one of the teenagers there. "Hey, Treg! I hope you and your family are doing well. I just wanted to let you know I was thinking about y'all and wanted to say hello. I also wanted to tell you something. When God called you somewhere else, I was pretty angry with you, mainly because I didn't understand. I do now, and forgiveness is something that's been big in my mind lately, and I wanted to ask you to forgive me for that."

Transitioning ministries is tough. As a pastor, you know how challenging and painful it can be when someone leaves your church. You almost feel betrayed or slighted. Now imagine how much stronger those feelings can be when it's the pastor who leaves.

Three states, three ministries, three senior pastors, and 11 homes later, let's just say I have transitioned a few times. Our first transition took us 450 miles south from what we knew as home. I still remember unloading the U-Haul in North Carolina and the church family making fun of my snow shovel. They were wondering just how big my dog was. Three years later, we were driving a U-Haul 350 miles back to the north, thankful we kept the snow shovel. Moving is death. Tears, heartache, uncertainty, hard feelings, misunderstanding, and packing and unpacking are horrible.

So, when do you leave a ministry? Or possibly a better question is this: How do you know when it is time to leave a ministry? Let me make it simple. You'll know when God tells you to. Sorry, I couldn't resist.

That opens up another question. How do I know when God is telling me to leave a ministry? God always makes it clear. As we seek Him and wait on Him, He opens and closes doors in our lives. God promises to lead us on a plain path (Prov. 3:5–6).

God begins His work with the still small voice of suggestion through the Spirit in our hearts. We begin to become unsettled and start to wonder what God is doing. I often say when people describe being in a transition stage that "God is shaking the tree." We are comfortable (at least we thought we were) in our current nest, and God begins to shake the tree ever so slightly, causing us to begin looking and wondering where we might land.

I spent two weeks in South Africa ministering and serving the Lord. I was in my 14th year of ministry, and my primary focus had always been on student ministries. Being in Africa gave me a new perspective. I was able to teach and train leaders in the church. I spent hours with pastors, counseling and encouraging each other. I was able to speak on various occasions and work with several outreach ministries. I came home knowing this was my calling. It was time to begin praying about transition ministries. I didn't know where or how, but I knew it would be soon.

Why? God was shaking the tree. "Delight thyself also in the LORD: and he shall give thee the desires of thine heart" (Ps. 37:4).

I am a firm believer that God is a desire-enabler. He plants desires in our hearts as we serve Him. When I began to desire another ministry, God was preparing me to leave. Now that we have covered the more philosophical, let's talk practical. Here are some things to consider as you try to understand if it is time for you to stay or go.

First, let's examine some reasons why you *shouldn't* leave. Then we'll look at all the reasons you should duck and run.

You Should Not Leave . . .

1. For Bigger and Better

Granted, your next move might be for bigger and better, but please don't make that your sole mission. More significant opportunities, expanded ministry, and more excellent pay are definitely something to consider but are not keywords for God's will.

Men are leaving ministries for bigger and better all the time. I recently heard a young man seek counsel from an older pastor about a move. The older pastor said, "You'll never get a chance to pastor a church that large again. You'd better say yes."

When was the last time you heard about a pastor leaving his current ministry and going to a much smaller church? You probably haven't. Don't get me wrong, bigger and better opportunities are not wrong, but with them come greater responsibilities. As shepherds—and we are responsible for our sheep—the bigger the flock, the greater the responsibility.

When I was an assistant, I received several phone calls a year from churches that were offering me an opportunity to either serve as a pastor or an assistant. In all but one case, it was either bigger or better—at least from the outside. In each case, God closed the door, and I now know why He did.

2. **For Open Doors**

On the heels of bigger and better are open doors. "God opened this door, and we had to take it." I have heard countless people say this. I always wonder what closed door they are running from. Or they say, "God has opened this door, and we must explore it."

I use the open-door analogy at times, but it isn't biblically rooted. The two open doors in Revelation 3:8 and 19 cannot possibly be talking in context about whether you should leave your current ministry. We cannot base decisions on open doors.

3. **Due to Difficult Times**

We are often tempted to leave when we are in a tough season. We all face rough seasons of ministry. We all have days, weeks, and months that we wish we were somewhere else. As you sit on the beaches of Hawaii, there are days that a church in Alaska doesn't sound all that bad (okay, that might be a stretch).

Difficult times will follow you wherever you go. Alaska or Hawaii, God allows those times to come to mold us and shape us. They are often precisely what we need to prepare us for the next step God has for us. They shouldn't cause us to run.

4. **To Prove a Point**

I've seen guys leave or threaten to leave to make a statement something like this: "If I leave, the church will see how bad things must be here and deal with the pastor." Or they might say, "If I leave, I know what that will do to our people, and they will see that the deacons are the problem." They even might say, "If I leave, this ministry will fall apart, and then they will see how essential I was to this work." God does not need you; He is simply choosing to use you by His grace.

5. **To Make Things Better**

It is not your church or ministry. Therefore, it is not your obligation to fix anything. It's God's. It always has been. It always will be. Chances are that after you leave, things will continue as before. Personality conflicts have split many staff members. Now that we know why we shouldn't leave, here are some reasons we should stay.

You Should Leave If . . .

Hold on! If you are eagerly anticipating this section—or perhaps, you even skipped the other chapters so you can find one reason to leave—stop! If you are contemplating leaving your current ministry but aren't sure why, email me. Let's talk about it.

1. **Immorality**

You should leave when something unethical or immoral is going on and it's not being dealt with. If you know your pastor is mishandling funds and you've done all you can to no avail, you might consider leaving. If you know your pastor is having an affair and people are turning a blind eye, leave.

Allow me to inject a spiritual warning. Leave if the Bible is not being taught and the pastor is just pounding out Saturday night specials. Your family needs to be fed spiritually. The preaching of God's Word should be a highlight of your week.

2. **Poverty**

You should leave when you can no longer feed your family. Remember what Paul said to Timothy—that a man who doesn't provide for his own household is worse than an infidel (1 Tim. 5:8). You have the moral and spiritual obligation to provide for and feed your family. When you accepted this position, you were possibly young and single. Now you're married with eight kids and making the same amount of money. It just isn't working out. It's time to move on.

Jimmy didn't want to leave, but there was no time in his schedule to have another job or side hustle. The church was understaffed, and he was doing the work of two assistants but underpaid as one. He finally decided to approach the board. Due to inflation going up significantly, the church's budget, and his growing family, he knew the only way he was going to make it financially was to get a part-time job. He hoped one of the pastors above him who was collecting Social Security, income revenues from IRAs, and a paycheck from the church would offer to take a pay cut so Jimmy could at least feed his family and keep his current obligations. Despite what Jimmy had hoped, the board agreed it was time for him to get a job. He was disappointed, but his wife was thrilled. She knew that would finally give them the finances they needed for their family. After the news of Jimmy's second job hit the congregation, it blew up in a very negative way. People were so upset that many of them asked the senior pastor when *he* was getting a job. Another meeting was called, and Jimmy was told he was not allowed to get a side job. He was also told the finances were not there for him to get a raise. He was stuck. It was time to leave.

3. **Pressure**

You should leave when the pastor or board makes it impossible to stay. Sometimes you need to read between the lines. Pastors have a unique way of not firing people. They force the assistant's hand to quit and then play the victim by telling people, "I don't know what happened. I didn't see that coming. I know I haven't allowed him to preach in the last six months or had time to meet with him, but to leave—what a shock!"

It is easier for you to leave than for the senior pastor to let you go. When you have no desire to leave, the pastor must find a way to make it happen. He will begin to give you reasons not to stay. This is just as sickening as when you know you can't stay, or maybe it's worse. This happened when David was playing his harp, and Saul decided it was time for him to go. But instead of spears, we often see these scenarios:

- *When your preaching time gets taken away from you.* If you preached once a month or every other week and suddenly you are not preaching as often as you once did, take heed.
- *When the pastor's disposition suddenly changes.* Watch your back if you find the pastor is not as friendly as he used to be. If the two of you had at least a weekly conversation and now he never has time to talk, start

buying moving boxes. If he makes a motion to the finance committee that your youth or other activity budget be lowered or unavailable, it is time to dust off your resume.
- *When everything you do is either wrong or not good enough.* Look out!
- *"People" are saying they are just not happy with you.* When the phrases "some parents," "some members," or "the board" are being used repeatedly to express the senior pastor's complaints, you have no future there.

Carey was either not willing or chose not to see these signs. In light of that, the pastor chose to hurt him—and to hurt others through him. Carey wanted to take his youth group to a Christian camp, but he knew most of his students' parents would never be able to afford it. He talked to the pastor about using the youth budget to help, but the pastor said the funds would not be used for camp. Instead, the pastor suggested doing fundraisers for camp. Carey worked himself to death for those kids that year. He operated many fundraisers to help raise money for his youth group to go to camp. It was two weeks before camp, and he had all the funds he needed. Everyone was so excited that they were able to go to camp. Then Cary received a strange call from the secretary that week. She told Carey the pastor wanted him to know that the financial books closed early that year. When he asked what that meant, she said, "The money in your fundraising account has been transferred to the church's general budget, and it is no longer available. I'm sorry, Carey, but the pastor said that money has now become a blessing to the church."

- *When it is the right move for your family.* Listen carefully. Your children and your wife are vital. You must decide to stay or go based on your family unit. I've watched pastors leave their current ministries to go to another opportunity and then lose their kids. I've seen pastors stay too long and watch their children grow bitter toward the ministry and leave the church as adults. Don't make that mistake.

Scriptural Examples
1. When It Is a Church-Led Decision

"Then pleased it the apostles and elders with the whole church, to send chosen men of their own company to Antioch with Paul and Barnabas; namely, Judas surnamed Barsabbas and Silas, chief men among the brethren" (Acts 15:22).

There will be certain cases when the whole church looks at their pastor, one of their pastors, or a member and says, "We can see where you would be a great missionary one day," or "Have you ever thought about planting a church?" Even though we might be second-guessing ourselves or our abilities, the Spirit of God is allowing the church to confirm that in you.

If my Spirit is confirming the guidance of the church, I would pack up my bags and go.

2. When God Closes All Doors

"Now, when they had gone throughout Phrygia and the region of Galatia, and were forbidden by the Holy Ghost to preach the word in Asia, after they were come to Mysia, they assayed to go into Bithynia: but the Spirit suffered them not" (Acts 16:6–7).

I can read the frustration between the lines of this passage. The previous verse talks about how churches were being established and growing, and now, of all times, God hits the brakes. I can hear Paul praying, "God, what are we doing? I don't understand why You are keeping us stuck here."

Why?

Macedonia was not quite ready. God knew in His wisdom and providence that the gospel needed to go west. When the time was right, God made sure Paul knew. God will make sure He lets you know when and where He wants you to go. You must learn to wait on Him. David encourages us with this in Psalm 27:14: "Wait on the Lord: be of good courage, and he shall strengthen thine heart: wait, I say, on the Lord."

You will never go wrong waiting. Imagine if Paul had not. Humanly speaking, we would be missing several books of our Bible, including Philippians. The gospel would have filtered through Asia and the East and never reached the West.

3. **In Times of Contention**

Here is one of the most shocking phrases in the Bible: "And the contention was so sharp between them" (Acts 15:39). I hate this! We read this passage and move on but imagine this happening in your home church. Some of you might not need to imagine. You might have seen something like this. It is devastating. Yet God in His wisdom can take a situation like this, turn it around, and use it for His glory. Again, I am not saying to run when a disagreement occurs, but when the contention is so much that it seems there is no resolving it, pray about moving on.

Would Paul have been as strongly persuaded to bring on Timothy (Acts 16:1–2) if Barnabas were still on the team? I highly doubt it. Would the people of Lystra and Iconium have encouraged Timothy to make this move had they not heard Paul had just lost one of his companions? Probably not.

God knows. It could be that you are reading this book right now because things are not good between you and the pastor, or you as the pastor and your assistant. That is okay. God could be using that right now to encourage you to move on and for someone else to move into your spot at the church.

Additional Thoughts

1. Staying in a ministry for a long period has many benefits. Being in a few different ministries also has benefits. Warren Wiersbe once said that God had him on a decade calendar. He was at each ministry for about 10 years. I would not be where I am and who I am without my three different ministries in three different states. Without all three, I would not have been able to write this book or minister to hundreds of assistants with my podcast.
2. It's very dangerous to tell someone in ministry that it's time for them to go. It's equally dangerous to tell someone they must stay when God leads them to go. I remember when we were preparing to visit another ministry. A few of my friends knew the purpose of the trip, and they came to visit. It wasn't to talk me into leaving; they all insisted I stay.

3. Leaving stinks. Pastor Chuck Swindoll, in his book *Saying It Well* (I recommend that you read it), talked about when he was leaving the East Coast for Texas. A little lady in the church came over to the window of their station wagon just as they were pulling out and said, "God showed me this was not his will." Pastor H. B. Charles said it was extremely difficult when they left their ministry (yes, for a larger one). The people gave him and especially his wife a very difficult time.
4. A wrong move does not mean you are useless. Poor John Mark in Scripture. Chances are he made the wrong move. He quit. He went home. He threw in the towel. I am sure he regretted leaving. He would have done things differently if given the chance. Despite this, John Mark didn't quit. He allowed his uncle to mentor him. He took advantage of his current home church location and studied under Peter's leadership. Thank the Lord he did. He was the only man that both Peter and Paul mentioned by name in the Bible as a valuable asset to their ministries.

As I reflected on this chapter, I opened an old journal to recall some of my days as an assistant. I found this entry: "Highlight of my day. We were talking about what envelope the money to pay for the McDonald's snack should come from (we had no money). My four-year-old said, 'I know, you can use the birthday money I just got!'"

We were a growing family and knew something had to change. Eventually, it did, and my journal then says, "How God brought my family to this point seems amazing! God has been *too* good. Kids love the new house and seem to love it here."

God knows. He is at work. Don't allow yourself to be blinded, though, by the circumstances around you. Do what you must, but never forget that God is on your side and will fight for you.

TIME TO REFLECT

1. Why are you still serving in the church and ministry you are currently in?
2. Are there any red flags that seem to be saying it is time to go? If so, what are they?
3. How would a move now positively or negatively affect your wife and children?

Art of Dealing with Criticism

"Pastor, we have been coming to your church for several weeks, and we will not be back. Your people are not welcoming at all, and we don't feel accepted here." One week earlier, another couple said, "Pastor, your church was so friendly. We felt welcomed and loved, and we didn't know anyone when we walked in. Thanks for having such a loving church."

We all love our critics—yeah, right! If you've been in ministry longer than about a week, you've probably gotten similar feedback. And it's probably been all over the map. Just look up Google reviews of my church and Christian school, and you will be entertained for hours.

It's healthy to be able to laugh a little because the truth is that critics have a way of getting under your skin. One negative review, comment, or post has the power to eliminate 50 positive comments you might receive. Critics have crushed the spirit and drive of many. Critics are quick to judge, extremely opinionated, and obviously "experts" in their field of choice.

Thom Rainer published an article regarding criticism of pastors. His opening paragraph is a quote from a criticized pastor. "There is a group of former church members in my community," the pastor said, "that is causing me great pain. They are regularly posting negative and divisive words on Facebook about my church, my family, and me. I have engaged them twice, and it only got worse. When you wrestle with a dirty pig, you get dirty yourself."

I talked to a pastor recently who is possibly one of the smartest men I know in ministry. He told me a member of his church asked to meet with the deacons and proceeded to tell them that the pastor either needed to be fired or have a mental health examination. If *he* has mental issues, I'm beyond hope.

If you have been in any position of leadership, from coaching your kid's soccer team to the president of an organization, you know what it is to wrestle with a "dirty pig." As hard as we try, it is impossible to keep everyone happy. Just ask a leader who had to decide regarding masks or no masks in 2020.

It often seems that no matter what decision you make, it causes contention. As a leader, you must make difficult decisions, even if that opens you up to criticism. Pastors aren't completely innocent in this arena either. Often, the pastor's relationship to criticism is like the man who owed money in the New Testament. He didn't want his creditors to be hard on him, but he made it miserable for others. Pastors err many times by giving undue criticism. We are critical. I am not sure how that seems to be every pastor's spiritual gift, but it is. We are critical of the church, the building, the choir, the song leader, the live stream, the parking lot, and even the way the mail was stacked on our desk.

There are times when criticism must be delivered, and when it is, there are some things you must keep in mind.

Delivering Constructive Criticism

1. **Take your criticisms directly to the person and not to everyone else around them.**

If you have a staff member on the team who is lazy, and if it feels like you are continually doing his work plus yours, go to him directly. You do not need to be bad-mouthing him to others behind his back. Paul could have easily bad-mouthed Peter to the Gentiles for his favoritism toward the Jews. Instead, Paul did what we all should do in this situation. He took the issue up with Peter. Paul says, "I withstood him to the face" (Gal. 2:11).

Pastor Lonnie was like all good youth pastors in charge of the annual Vacation Bible School. This year, Lonnie was going to try to change things up a bit. He was going to invite some kids from the community. Historically, VBS had just been a week-long babysitting service for the parents at Stonebrook Church. Kids in the community would require more work and attention, and it was not worth the effort—but not this year. Lonnie was willing to shake it up for the cause of the gospel.

His efforts did not completely fail. Two kids from the neighborhood showed up. Their parents would not bring them, so they rode bikes to VBS. The pastor did not share in Lonnie's excitement. "Watch those kids," he told Lonnie. "We don't want anything stolen from the church this week."

Lonnie did watch them. He took them on as his personal project. On Thursday of that week, one of the kids ended up pushing his bike to church. His chain had fallen off, and he told Lonnie he could not fix it. Game time was pretty well handled by the members of Stonebrook, so Lonnie took Gabe aside and not only fixed his bike for him but showed him how he could fix it if it happened again.

The pastor was watching this whole event transpire. He approached one of the board members who was helping with the games. The pastor said, "Look at Lonnie. I told him these neighborhood kids would just be trouble. Am I paying him to run a VBS or a bike repair shop?" The next day, Lonnie heard all about it, unfortunately not from the pastor but at lunch with that board member. That opened Lonnie's eyes (or at least made him aware) of what the pastor honestly thought about him and his ministry. From that moment until he moved on, Lonnie looked at his senior pastor in a different light and remained insecure in their relationship.

2. Consider what it might do to the one receiving it.

You need to take into account the personality, strengths, and weaknesses of the person you are about to deliver the criticism to. Make sure to bring their strengths into the conversation, preferably first, before going into their weaknesses.

Consider the above illustration with Lonnie. The pastor should have taken Lonnie to lunch the next day and said, "Lonnie, I love your heart for people and how you go the extra mile to make everyone feel welcome. I love the extra time you have taken with neighbor kids and their spiritual needs. But allow me to run something by you. Last night during craft time, we were shorthanded and needed all available adults helping. I know Cole was probably too old for the craft, and that is why he was working on his bike, but I needed you at that time as well. Do you understand what I'm saying? Next time just tell Cole that you'll be happy to help him work on his bike—but only after VBS is over."

Now, no feelings are hurt. Lonnie is not discouraged from doing what he does best, and he understands there are times when his gifts need to be put in check.

I was at Dunkin' Donuts last week (I know, big surprise), and the woman working not only gave me my coffee but a free donut as well. I knew right then it was going to be a good day. She said it was for being so nice and patient. She then told me a story about a man who got very upset with her last month. She said he wrote an awful review and called corporate on her. She was in tears as she told me the story. I just wanted to give the poor woman a hug and my donut back (not really). This one act of criticism crushed her. If you are so self-consumed that you fail to think of the one you are about to criticize, keep your comments to yourself. A good rule of thumb is to never say anything online or elsewhere about a person that you wouldn't be willing to say to them face to face.

3. **Prayerfully ask God to search your heart to ensure the criticism is not coming from a heart of jealousy or selfishness.**

It is amazing how critical we can be of someone else's ministry when we are actually jealous of the growth and success they are having. We all have chinks in our armor, but we might be focusing on that weakness because the strengths that pastor exhibits in all other areas of his life drive you crazy.

Pray and check your heart. A heart check in prayer is necessary before any conversation that is likely to include constructive criticism. Be sure your feedback comes from right motives.

Opposing someone face-to-face can be and is often a terrible process. Being the one receiving it is even worse. It is humbling and at times discouraging to find out we are not perfect. No one likes to have their weaknesses pointed out. Even the thoughts of sending this book off to the editor scares me to death. My perfect manuscript is about to be destroyed, and my feelings are going to be hurt.

Receiving Criticism

If you're on the receiving end of criticism (constructive or otherwise), here are some tips to help you mentally prepare for it.

1. **Consider the source.**

Look closely at the past and present circumstances in the critic's life. It could be that you wrote, talked about, or otherwise touched on something that hit a nerve. You might have provided a way for them to vent their hurt caused by other life issues. Criticism can be an external response to an internal scar that runs deep in them. So, ask yourself if this is a person who tends to kick even when they are not swimming. Do they complain about everything?

If so, there is nothing you can do in a situation like that. You can try to kill them with kindness, but doing so might not be worth your time, effort, or energy.

2. **Make sure the critic is not calling the shots.**

Criticism can often be nothing more than an attempt to control. This is especially troubling for leaders who tend to put way too much value on the thoughts of the minority while neglecting the majority. Most of us focus on the few who critique us instead of the majority who support us. Basing your motives and actions on their possible reactions is not leading; it is being led.

Many times, our first reaction to criticism is a desire to quit. If I were to quit every time I was criticized, I would be in my 20th house instead of my 11th. We can't do that. A pastor friend of mine once said. "I've had people tell me to use more family illustrations and to never use family illustrations on the same day for the same sermon. I've gotten texts that a sermon was loved and hated. People have left our church because of a word they thought I said."

I love what President Lincoln said regarding this. "I do the very best I know how—the very best I can; and I mean to keep doing so until the end. If the end brings me out all right, what's said against me won't amount to anything. If the end brings me out wrong, ten angels swearing I was right would make no difference."

3. **Ask God to help you receive it with meekness.**

Faithful are the wounds of a friend. I know no one who enjoys receiving solid criticism, but if done correctly, I know no one who has yet to learn valuable lessons from it.

In my first ministry, there was someone with a PhD. He was a fantastic man. I loved and still love him and his wife.

He usually had a word of criticism about my sermon but was always gracious in his delivery. He never criticized my content but normally had a few suggestions about the southeastern Ohio language I was using. For instance, "Treg, you keep saying 'at' at the end of your questions." He was the first to inform me that "where you at" is not proper English. I love him for caring enough to help me become a better public speaker.

When Criticism Hurts

Let's say the criticism hurts. It was handled in the wrong spirit, and you feel like it was much more of an attack than constructive suggestions. Often, that is the case. Consider these thoughts before you go after that person with a flying fist.

1. **Take it to Jesus.**

First and foremost, we must take it to the Lord with an open mind and based on the Bible. I love how Nehemiah dealt with the criticism from Sanballat and Tobiah. He took it straight to God in prayer. "My God, think thou upon Tobiah and Sanballat according to these their works, and on the prophetess Noadiah, and the rest of the prophets, that would have put me in fear" (Neh. 6:14).

2. **Confront it.**

Second, confront the issue head-on. If you can't let it go, then go to them. Granted, some issues will not be worth pursuing, but if you must, go to them directly (Matt. 25:23–24). If you are in a public office or ministry, you can't live your life on the defense. You must learn to move on and let the haters hate.

3. **Don't take it home.**
I know this third one is much easier said than done. Your family does not need to be carrying the load of such things. Leave the burden of the criticism in the office or the car. Don't allow it to cross your threshold. Protect your family and those closest to you.

I will not tell my wife about the criticism I receive. Your wife does not need the emotional hurt and anger toward that person when she sees them in church on Sunday. You know your wife loves you and would defend you, so why test her loyalty?

Sometimes, the hurt and the criticism creep into your home. No matter what you do, it is unavoidable. I remember when my youngest daughter found the not so nice reviews about our church and Christian school on Google reviews. A few employees I have had to let go over the years have made their thoughts of me known (under fake names, of course). This was extremely hard on my daughter.

4. **Love your enemy.**
Fourth, do your best to give your critics fist bumps, not fists to the face. When you see them at the store, don't switch aisles. Make them switch aisles. Always smile and shake their hand, do a fist bump, or do whatever we do these days. I know your flesh wants to react and put this person in their place. They might even deserve it. Don't do it. *Don't!* Don't succumb to their level. Don't satisfy them with a response. "Therefore if thine enemy hunger, feed him; if he thirst, give him drink: for in so doing thou shalt heap coals of fire on his head" (Rom. 12:20). I'm not exactly sure what it means to heap coals of fire, but I think

I know enough to apply it the best I can. Christ said, "Love your enemies, bless them that curse you, do good to them that hate you, and pray for them which despitefully use you, and persecute you" (Matt. 5:44).

Finally, allow me to caution you to be careful about how much of this you share with your pastor. If it is serious, he will find out eventually, or perhaps he already knows. I have seen pastors allow these words of criticism to darken their thinking about you and your ministry. His attitude toward you and your work could go south in a hurry.

Adrian found this out the hard way. He could not believe what he was hearing. Did someone in the church genuinely hate him that much? How could someone have the time to pick apart everything he did? This person even went so far as to write in a letter that the pastor made a mistake in hiring him. That was not even the worst of it. He criticized his wife's "fake" smile and overt friendliness. While the pastor was reading this, Adrian burst out in anger and self-defense, demanding to know who wrote it. The pastor would not give him an answer and actually should not have read the letter to him. How could someone have the courage to write such accusations?

How could they be so brave in writing yet so cowardly in not going to Adrian directly? The pastor told Adrian not to worry about it, to take from it what he could, and to move on. Yeah, right! Adrian never forgot those words. They were like a black cloud that followed him for the rest of his ministry there. According to the letter (rather, because of his response to it), he was never able to feel accepted, knowing that people saw him and his wife that way.

When It Comes from Your Boss

Now, let's take it even one step closer to home. How do we handle criticism when it comes straight at us across from the pastor's (or boss's) desk?

Listen

In this situation, let me encourage you to listen actively and attentively. Pay attention to what your boss is saying and ask questions if needed. Don't interrupt to defend yourself, and never become defensive. It's not easy to receive criticism, but it's important to keep an open mind and consider the feedback objectively. Try to see things from the pastor's perspective and determine why your boss felt it was important to share with you.

Grow

Criticism can also be a valuable opportunity for growth and improvement. Look for the constructive aspects of the criticism and use them to identify areas for improvement.

Grace

The way you respond is extremely important. I still remember a conversation I had to have with a staff member about his attitude toward another employee. We went out for coffee to discuss it. As we arrived back at the church, I finished the conversation by saying I believed he was wrong and should prayerfully consider apologizing. As I stepped out of the car, he left in such a rage that he squealed his tires as he left. If you jump to your own defense and lose your cool, everything you have done up to that point is pointless.

When responding to criticism, it's also important to do so respectfully. When the critic has finished, thank the person delivering the criticism for their time and willingness to approach you face-to-face. Let the person know you appreciate their input and will prayerfully consider everything they said. If you disagree with the criticism (and the situation requires that you voice your disagreement), do so politely.

Explanation

If you feel you must explain things from your perspective, be careful. Criticism typically points at weaknesses and blind spots. Our minds need time to comprehend the criticism and weigh its legitimacy. Take all the time you need to process what you have heard. The amygdala in your brain goes into fight-or-flight mode in these situations, so an instantaneous response tends to be unmeasured and ungracious. Take the time to go on a long run, a walk, or a bike ride if you can. You need to release that stimulation on something instead of someone.

I received a text message recently from a member who made a terrible accusation about me and the ministry. It was hard to process, mainly because I considered him a friend. I received the text on Saturday and did not respond until early Monday morning. I'm glad I waited. It not only allowed me to cool off but let him see the wrong in his explosive actions.

You can never go wrong taking as much time as you need to process criticism before responding. Give yourself space to reflect on the feedback, and then consider your responses carefully. Don't rush into a response you may later regret.

Dealing with criticism can be challenging, but doing so is essential for personal and professional growth. We all dislike criticism, but we need to begin processing these steps so we know how to deal with it when it comes. If you become defensive or angry, always apologize and ask forgiveness for your actions.

TIME TO REFLECT

1. What has been the most difficult criticism you ever received? What was it about that particular criticism that upset you most? Why did you take it so personally?
2. Think back on the last time you criticized someone online. If that person were to walk up to you today, would you still say the same thing? Why or why not?
3. Write a note to someone who criticized you in the past. Be honest with them about how it made you feel, but then thank them. Let them know you understand that it could not have been easy for them to approach you in that way and how you have grown from it. You might be surprised how much better you will feel toward that person and yourself once you do that.

Art of Discipleship

Stepping into the doors of our quaint little church as a kid, my eyes would light up at the sight of a projector perched on a sheet of plywood laid over the pews. This setup signaled a thrilling thing: a missionary was visiting. The nostalgic click of the old slides transported us to far-off places, even if it sometimes meant turning our heads upside down to view the occasional misplaced slide.

I do not remember each slide or every missionary, but one image remains etched in my memory. It was often the final slide of the presentation that usually depicted a breathtaking sunset over the mission field. This poignant image was frequently accompanied by Matthew 9:37–38: "Then saith he unto his disciples. The harvest truly is plenteous, but the labourers are few; pray ye therefore the Lord of the harvest, that he will send forth labourers into his harvest."

How could this be the end of the slide show? Why was there never a follow-up picture? Countless times we were left pondering the sunset and the encroaching darkness over that distant field. Those slides failed to show that in just a few hours, the sun would rise again, heralding a new day and new ways God desired to work.

What was the work? What was it Jesus was specifically asking them to pray about, and what drove Him to pray through the night (Luke 6:12)? He was launching a mentorship program. "And when it was day, he called unto him his disciples; and of them he chose twelve, whom also he named apostles" (Luke 6:13, cf. Matt. 10:1).

The sun arose with the next generation of church planters. It arose with the future. It arose upon 12 men who eventually would be accused of turning the world upside down for Jesus.

I am convinced we are watching the "sunset" and darkness fall on many ministries, organizations, and churches today because they are not praying about and investing in the next generation. They have failed to follow these principles and those of 2 Timothy 2:2 and Titus 2:3–5.

Mentoring is essential. Mentoring is our calling. I have been asked to be a mentor many times over the years and twice already this summer. Despite a busy schedule, it is difficult to say no. Why? Because it is important to the future of the church. Sharing life with others is a fantastic opportunity. Being able to pour into the life of another is a calling and a great responsibility. Helping a person grow as a leader, mentor, or parent is also a tremendous blessing.

What is a mentor? A mentor is someone who pours into the life of another and guides them in a specific direction. People often think of a mentor as someone to tell them what to do, but that is not the case. Simon Sinek, author and inspirational speaker, is correct when he says, "A mentor is not someone who walks ahead of us and tells us how they did it. A mentor walks alongside us to guide us on what we can do." Entrepreneur and author Jim Rohn says this: "My mentor said, 'Let's go do it,' not 'You go do it.' How powerful when someone says, 'Let's!'"

Taking a younger or even older person under your tutelage and investing in them does not have to be a difficult task or undertaking. You do not have to be someone who has accomplished great accolades or tremendous success, wisdom, or ability. It does not require you to be a master teacher.

Jesus was the perfect example of a mentor. He did not choose 12 men to sit under his seminary training, nor did he choose them to emulate Him. Jesus chose 12 men to mentor. Mark says this: "And he ordained twelve, that they should be with him" (Mark 3:14).

Did you catch that? Mentorship means time together. If you want to see the sunrise on your church, ministry, or organization, it is time to start praying for and pursuing someone you can "ordain" to mentor. We have a mentorship (fellowship) program that allows us to bring a young man in to be mentored. I am mentoring several men now. I am praying about the next young man God will have for us. Why? It is essential. It is our calling.

Coach John Wooden once said, "A good coach can change a game. A great coach can change a life." Whose life are you changing today to change the future of tomorrow? I'm afraid many pastors' answer would be a blank stare.

In a self-survey I did among pastors a few years ago, 70 percent of pastors said they felt like they were not mentored properly to prepare them for the ministry. Actually, I am not sure anyone is fully ready to step into the head pastor role, but I do know they are not ready if they have not had proper discipleship and mentoring. The position of pastor lends itself to pride and arrogance. If a young man has the desire to wear a cape and his underwear outside his pajamas, kryptonite will follow him wherever he goes. Or if he prefers chaps, boots, and a cowboy hat, along with a six-shooter, he will find himself hanging his hat from many locations in his lifetime. There is no place for cowboys or heroes in God's ministry—only shepherds.

Living in a college town with a good medical program and a major hospital, I have had the opportunity to meet several doctors, residents, and fellows. These men and women immediately have my respect. The amount of time, energy, and effort they have put into their studies to get where they are is a major accomplishment. A few years ago, a vascular surgeon started attending our church. He was in his mid-30s and still "learning." He was at West Virginia University as a fellow. He would study under the head vascular surgeon for two years before he could go out on his own. He already had eight years of schooling and four years of residency, but he still had two years to go.

Why do we think we can send men out into the ministry with no formal training after a basic four-year degree? Our calling is like no other. We watch over people's souls. We are required to rightly divide the Word and feed the flock. I wasn't ready (though I thought I was) at 22. Very few are. New shepherds need to be taught both by example and instruction. Each man must give an account for his actions, but I am afraid many pastors are to blame for the failures we are seeing in the next generation of leaders. Before this can happen, though, a person must be willing to be mentored.

Be a Disciple

Paul said, "Be ye followers of me, even as I also am of Christ" (1 Cor. 11:1). My favorite discipleship verse says, "And he ordained [appointed] twelve, that they should be with him, and that he might send them forth to preach" (Mark 3:14). Why did Jesus choose them? He wanted them to be with him. Much of discipleship is just being with people—on road trips, while sitting by the lake, at every chance you get.

Christ was with His disciples. He walked with them, laughed with them, and took every opportunity to pour Himself into them. Mentors are necessary and extremely important in all areas of life. Who we learn from plays a crucial role in who we become. Most of us can look back on our elementary days and name at least one teacher who made an impact on our lives and influenced us toward the path we eventually chose. Steve Jobs, talking about his fourth-grade teacher, said, "I learned more from her than any other teacher, and if it hadn't been for her, I'm sure I would have gone to jail." "Teddy," as he called her, put extra time and energy into Steve that set him on a course to eventually develop the device I am typing on right now.

Politicians, pastors, media celebrities, and others who have found themselves in the spotlight with not enough time in the shadows often end up in failure. Without following or being mentored by a respected leader before the lights, camera, and action, many novices find themselves on the path to destruction. God uses a slow cooker, not a microwave, for his leaders. We see microwaved men and women burning out and falling apart way too soon in our churches and ministries.

Paul told the church at Corinth to follow him. He told the church at Philippi to do the things they had learned, received, and heard from him. He told Timothy to take the things he had learned from Paul (as a follower) and commit them to other faithful men (followers) who would do the same.

Paul knew that for the ministry to continue, he would need to mentor sons in the faith. Demas left the race, but Paul encouraged Timothy in his last letter to stay the course. I love how Fadee Andrawos illustrates this in his blog on *Medium*:

> Think of a 4x400m relay race. The first man ran a great leg, and he passed the baton to the second man, who was way ahead, and he made a perfect pass to the third. And the third guy walks off and sits on the grass. His excuse? I didn't feel like running. You didn't feel like it? You can't do that! Timothy, you are a link in a chain, and you need to both guard the purity of the treasure and then pass it on. You are a link in a relay race, and someone is waiting for you to give them the baton. You can't just sit down. It's not up to you! The treasure has been invested in you, and you have to keep the truth going! More so in 2 Timothy 1:15, Paul describes unfaithful servants who stopped running. Who stopped teaching? And he includes these names to say, look, Timothy? Do you want to be like them? or do you want to be on my team and keep running?

Whose team do you desire to run with? What kind of team do you desire to lead? Do you want to be part of those who have been known to drop out and fail or those who are known for their faithfulness and loyalty to Christ? Even if I am currently being discipled, which at times we all should be, I need to also be continually fulfilling the command to make disciples.

Make Disciples

Timothy was not only required to be a disciple but also to make disciples. If you follow this pattern in Scripture, you will see how God used men to invest in others to make a major impact on the world. We know the Lord Jesus set this example when He took on the 12 disciples. He also limited them to three on various occasions. Moses saw the value in Joshua. God told Elijah to find Elisha. There is no better way for you to spend your time than investing in the lives of others. This is a principle found throughout the New Testament and early church history.

Peter saw an opportunity to invest in a young man named Mark (1 Pet. 5). Mark had a past and a reputation as a quitter and dissenter. He was the one everyone blamed for breaking up the dynamic duo of Paul and Barnabas. Talk about a rough Instagram bio! "John Mark. Quit the ministry. The great splitter-upper." Ouch! Peter, knowing Mark's past failures, saw an opportunity. If anyone could empathize with this young man, it was him. Peter knew what it felt like to be a deserter. He knew what it was like to have his loyalties questioned (John 21). Mark became such a valuable asset to Peter that he called him his son in his epistle. Paul even says in 2 Timothy 4:11 that he desires John Mark's company because he is profitable for the ministry. John Mark went on to write "Peter's Gospel," known to us as the Gospel of Mark.

The Apostle John did not waste his life doing his own thing either. History tells us that John poured his life into Polycarp, who then invested in one named Irenaeus, who trained a young Hippolytus. These four men did amazing things for the Kingdom. John's legacy outlived him for generations.

Parents, now is the time for you to make disciples of your children. Pastors, now is the time for you to build a church of disciple-makers. Christian, now is the time to start pouring your life into a young believer.

Assistants, now is not just the time for you to be mentored but also a time to start mentoring others. Now is the prime time to begin building relationships and making disciples within your community. Without the pressure of being the lead pastor, you are not necessarily needed in your office 24/7 and have some freedoms the pastor might not have. Your position as an associate allows you to enjoy friendships while setting an example. Find ways to be with people. Coach a sport. Do small group Bible studies. Just be with them, and go and make disciples.

Invest Wisely

When the stock market crashed in 2020, a few friends and I decided to jump in and buy up some stock. I invested $1,500 and ended up walking away with over $3,000. A 50 percent increase in income is really good. If I put an ad online and told people that I average a 25–50 percent return on all my investments, I would have a huge following. But it was not rocket science when the market hit an all-time low. I also purchased some stocks that went nowhere. I knew better, but I was hoping the no-name companies would go big. They didn't. I am still a few hundred dollars in the red with them, and I have my fingers crossed that they will miraculously rebound.

Eventually, I will probably need to cut my losses and walk away. A good friend of mine invested $5,000 in the stock market in March 2020. He was smarter than I (obviously, he's a surgeon) and only invested in secure companies that guaranteed dividends and were sure to rebound. Rebound they did. He made well over $10,000 with his investment.

I'm afraid my years of ministry have negatively influenced my investment strategies—in stocks and in people. I always try to find the underdog and believe they'll turn around. I say, "With the right amount of work and time, that girl can one day do great things for God." I claim, "He has so much potential if—." We so often look around the church and find the teens, college kids, or adults who really have a long way to go and invest all we have in them. They are running from God, but something inside of us is drawn to the challenge. Hours of time and money are spent on these investments with little to no return. We make ourselves sick over their failures and rejoice with the slightest victory. I have spent countless hours on these investments and have seen little return.

Let me encourage you to invest in the ones you know will yield a return, the ones you know will produce dividends in eternity. Find them, and invest in them. It is the average one that needs your help. It is the average, boring investment that will yield the largest increase with long-term investing. Find that boy or girl you see as average, and do all you can for them. The excellent ones will excel, and the rebellious ones will rebel, but with constant investment, the average ones could yield dynamic dividends. Start investing in the average, and watch them become great over time.

Do nothing without taking a disciple with you. You have the time and ability to take young people under your wing and develop them for service in the future. Over the years, countless college kids were found "doing life" with our family. In Ohio, we had teens or college kids with us continually. In North Carolina, college kids were in our home nearly all the time.

Here in West Virginia (the home of West Virginia University), we live among, with, and around college kids 24/7, and we love it. These young men and women are in such a formable time of life, and they need someone to be there when they are making decisions and looking for direction. They will one day move on to become members of another church, which is okay. So why should you invest in them? Because you can make sure they become an asset to a future pastor one day and not a liability. You can show young men and women how family life works. You can set an example outside the church walls of what a Christian home should look like. You can set an example of Christ in the home without opening a marriage or family book, or teaching a seminar.

I got permission from my wife to take some Christmas money and buy the *FIFA '17* video game. I couldn't wait to play it with some of the college guys. So, we invited a few of them over for dinner and some much-anticipated game time. While we were playing some serious soccer, my boys (ages seven and eight) were wrestling around the living room (nothing unusual). They bumped into the Xbox, and the game ejected the CD. We then started yelling as our game came to a sudden stop. To fix the problem, my oldest kicked the tray to put the disc back into the Xbox. The disc slid up on the tray, scratching it right down the middle and making it unusable. I was mad, but Carrie was furious. The college boys almost cried because they were so scared. This was real life, the real Spicer family. Lessons like this will be etched in those college kids' memories when their crazy kids do the same.

Be Intentional

Every Sunday night, we had the college kids over to our home for dinner and games. After dinner and a round or two of *Catan* or *Ticket to Ride,* we would turn on YouTube and watch the newest and most popular preachers discuss their sermons and theology. That allowed them to get my opinions and also allowed me to see and hear what the younger generation was being influenced by. We had several valuable talks and Bible studies in our living room on Sunday nights and early Monday mornings.

Most Sunday nights after church, these college kids headed to our home, grabbed the key hidden in the garage, and waited for us to get there. One Sunday evening, the key was missing, and they decided to climb through our bathroom window. The neighbor, not knowing what was going on, walked up behind them, and greeted them with his 12-gauge shotgun. They definitely needed the bathroom after that.

Today, I am more of a coffee shop pastor. I spend tons of time sipping coffee and discussing life and the Bible while building relationships. My modus operandi is to ask a lot of questions. I love asking questions. That is how I get to know people, who they are, and what makes them tick. Plus, a coffee shop setting is relaxed and non-confining. Once the coffee is done, you can grab a refill or leave, and that's okay. I also have made the golf course a relationship-building venue. I couldn't do this as an associate pastor because I was broke, and the pastor would never go for it. But if you have not taken a vow of poverty, this is the way to go. You have a captive audience on the golf course. Sitting in a cart for four hours provides great conversation and opportunities to share your testimony and ask pointed questions.

The main thing to remember about building relationships is to be intentional. It doesn't just happen. Christ constrained His disciples to go on the ship. He needed to go through Samaria. This was a disciple-making opportunity that Christ intentionally set up. You must be intentional when it comes to making appointments with people so you can invest in them.

Never Stop

When I started to compete in triathlons, I knew I needed to purchase a "real" triathlon bike. But I didn't just go buy one. I built one. I started with the frame and then the wheels, saddle, tires, and so on. One of the last purchases I made was the chain. I put it on and took my tri-bike out for the first time. It was amazing! I rode down my typical route and began my first climb. As I stood up and cranked the pedals, my chain popped off. The master link was not tight enough, and I was done instantly.

An evangelist who was speaking at our church brought with him a young man he was mentoring. I set up a two-hour time slot to pour myself into this 24-year-old man. When we were done, he said, "Pastor, I have been traveling for two years, and you are the first pastor to ever talk to me." This is unfortunate! The next generation of leaders is out there, and we are doing nothing about it.

This is why churches are dying. This is why fellowships are falling apart. The chain has been broken. Our young leaders are the master link to hold it together. Don't break the chain. "And the things that thou hast heard of me among many witnesses, the same commit thou to faithful men, who shall be able to teach others also" (2 Tim. 2:2). Was Paul just wanting them to hang out and teach in Ephesus? No. His desire was for them to go and teach in every city and replicate themselves.

Unfortunately, many pastors have broken the chain. They are too busy with programs, numbers, traveling, friends, and board meetings to make disciples. This is killing the next generation who is hungry to learn and needs someone to invest in them.

But Treg, you might be saying, I don't see myself in this ministry long-term. These college kids are only here for four years. I'm in a transient location. People come and go all the time. Isn't building relationships in these scenarios a waste of time? No!

God has not called us to sit and wait until the perfect ministry comes our way. You are where you are to make an impact on the others around you for eternity. I don't care if you will only be there for six months. Pour your life into someone during those six months. The college kids might move on, but so what? You have four years to pour yourself into them and see them leave, ready to replicate your teaching elsewhere.

This is our calling.

TIME TO REFLECT

1. Who is the last person you mentored? Where are they now?
2. As you read this chapter, who did God lay on your heart that you should invest in?
3. Who is someone you can call or a coach you can hire to invest in you today?

Art of Preaching

Robbie's ears perked up. He was positive he had heard or read about another man who interpreted Romans 3 the same way. He didn't think much of it but listened more intently to his pastor while trying to connect the dots. His mind waned after a few minutes of intense listening until it suddenly came back to life. His pastor was dealing with Romans 3:25 and said that "salvation is not primarily for your benefit; it is for the glory of God. We are a means to an end. We are not the end." *Hold on. I've heard that before*, Robbie thought. He could not wait for the sermon to end so he could get to work on who the mysterious commentator was. It did not take much effort to find that quote online. As he traced the quote back to the original sermon, Robbie found more than he bargained for. He could not believe what he was reading. His pastor didn't just quote Pastor John MacArthur without giving him credit, but he had quoted the entire sermon. A week had passed, and Robbie hadn't given much thought to the previous Sunday's sermon after the initial shock. And besides, weeks are crazy, schedules are continually changing, and his pastor could have just had a rough week and needed a little extra help. Now, as they turned to Romans again, Robbie heard familiar language and sentence structure again. He wasn't waiting this time. He grabbed his phone to find MacArthur's series on Romans chapter four. To his dismay, not only did he find it, but he was able to follow along almost word for word with his pastor.

Curt decided he would attend a specific youth rally with his son's youth group. He was unfamiliar with the speaker and wanted to hear him. As the man began to preach, Curt thought, "I preached a sermon with that title." You can imagine Curt's surprise when he realized the speaker was preaching his very sermon.

The stories of Robbie and Curt are not unique. This is a reality that is running rampant in pulpits across the country. With transcript-generating apps, resources such as Sermon Central and the incredible capabilities of artificial intelligence (AI), genuine sermons are rarer than you might think. Pastor Allistair Begg once said it seems silly that the only difference between plagiarizing and not plagiarizing is a footnote. He is right. There is nothing new under the sun, but we are also responsible to study to show ourselves approved unto God.

If you are doing what most assistant pastors do, I completely understand why you would be tempted to rely heavily on resources to help write your sermon. There are weeks when there is no spare time to add one more thing, especially sermon prep, to your schedule.

I landed at Faith Baptist Church in July 2014. The pastor I had come to serve under and eventually replace had been diagnosed with colon cancer just a few months prior. We were able to have a few months together before his cancer surgery on the first of September. He had only planned on being off work for about a week for recovery. Needless to say, a week was not quite long enough. It was eight months before he could return to church. In an approximately 24-hour period, I became the pastor, assistant pastor, school administrator, basketball coach, high school Bible teacher, grad school student, youth pastor, college pastor, and janitor. Oh yeah, I was also a husband and father of four.

Looking back, I wish I had had AI to help get me through some of those long weeks. I am not sure I could have done it, but would it have been wrong for me to read a MacArthur sermon on Sunday morning after an extremely long week?

Peter gives us the answer in his tribute to the elders in 1 Peter 5. He tells them that above all else, they need to shepherd the flock of God. How would they do that? I believe the translators of the King James version of the Bible nailed it when they wrote for verse two, "Feed the flock of God." Our flocks have specific nutritional needs and require specific items in their diets based on their geography and culture. We are required to give that to them. As I write this paragraph, I am looking out the window at rolling hills of vast farmlands. As I preach this weekend, my notes from my past Sunday sermon at Faith will not work here. Why? My college culture-crafted sermon would need some alteration before it would have any impact and meaning here.

Pastor, you have the command to feed the flock of God. If sheep are malnourished, they will eventually go where the food is despite the terrain or the difficult journey to find it. You want a fat flock. Every chance you get, feed them. Whether that is the lambs (children or youth ministry), the sheep, or the older sheep, you need to take this task of feeding seriously. You need to feed the sheep a big old Sunday morning feast every week. You have the privilege and responsibility to feed them a specially prepared meal you have had plenty of time to ponder, research, prepare, and produce.

I did not. It was grace that got me through many sermons. One Saturday while I was studying for grad school, I had a test that needed to be finished by midnight. I studied all day, took the test around 10:00 p.m., and then began to finalize my sermon for Sunday. I would write my Sunday school lesson on Sunday morning and my evening message on Sunday afternoon. It was not a good situation.

Why are so many guys pulling out the books, AI, or someone else's sermon on Saturday night? Are pastors just natural procrastinators? Do we do our best work when we are under pressure? I believe we rely too heavily on our abilities and way too little on the responsibility of teaching God's Word.

The Problem in Preparation
We Are the Problem

The first problem is you. Many of you will be tempted to skip this chapter when it comes to preaching because you know you know how to preach. I ask you, though, to keep reading. We all need a spirit of humility and a desire to learn like George. One Sunday evening, George sent me an email. He is an incredibly intelligent man who works for the Department of Defense doing things I am not allowed to know. He said, "I think I know what I know, but I know that I don't know what you know. Can we start meeting for coffee so I can learn what you know?"

Coffee and Jesus—it doesn't get much better than that, guys. I'm not saying I know it all, but I have messed up in this area so many times. Stay with me, and I will do my best to share what I know with you.

Our Ego Is a Problem

The second problem is your ego. As an assistant pastor, you have it made. Every time you preach, the congregation makes all over your delivery. You cruise right through your preaching sessions. You know the pastor is sitting there wishing he could preach like you.

But I promise you that preaching is not going to come that easily all the time. As your schedule begins to fill up or if the Lord puts you in the senior pastor role, you'll long for these days again.

Some of you know that feeling already. Not only will you have the weight of the ministry on you, but you also will have several other speaking engagements that fill your calendar. Everybody loves the new cowboy when he comes to town. Eventually, he becomes covered in dust and dirt like all the other cowboys and is overlooked.

Our Schedule Is a Problem

The third problem with preaching is the difficulty of keeping any series or expository sermons going. Will anyone remember what you preached last month? Will you even remember? Probably not. You can either review for several minutes or by default become more of a topical speaker. That's fine as long as you are preaching God's Word and have put the time and energy into it. I still remember sermons that guest speakers preached here on a

Sunday morning that were a great blessing. I also have files full of my one-shot wonders from years gone by.

The fourth problem is procrastination. You have several irons in the fire. You have a thousand responsibilities. When you can't imagine doing anything more, you receive a text message from the pastor that says, "I would like you to preach on Sunday." Normally, this is not a problem unless this text message comes on Thursday afternoon. These times give you no choice but to pray, lean on what you have been studying or reading, and rely on grace while getting a sermon together on Saturday.

Suppose you are one of those guys who wait until Saturday to get the ball rolling. Stop! Procrastination can pay off in certain areas of life, but when it comes to sermon prep, it cannot.

The Solution

You must change your schedule on the weeks you know you are preaching. Sermon prep must go to the top of your to-do list. Everything must revolve around this event. All other scheduled events that week need to be examined and, if possible, eliminated. Postpone or delegate, and get out the books.

I encourage you to take these sermons seriously. You have no idea the impact you can make with your words. As an assistant, you are much like a guest speaker or evangelist. You are a fresh voice. You are a loved pastor. You have energy and enthusiasm when you are behind the pulpit, much like the senior pastor once was in many cases. You have spontaneity going for you. You bat .400 every time.

Now that I have your ego built up, tap your cleats, and point the bat to the outfield. Put the bat away, Jose Canseco (showing my age here). Your natural abilities and energies will not compensate for the work only the Spirit of God can do. You need to look at preaching, even if it is only once a month, as a very serious event.

On the week you preach, your schedule needs blocks of time for sermon writing. Every morning when you wake and every night when you put your head on the pillow, your mind should be thinking about your sermon. A pastoral coach sat down with me several years ago and helped me develop this schedule. I am not saying this is a copy-paste solution. All of us are different and have a variety of schedules and responsibilities. I just want this to get you thinking about what your schedule could look like on these preaching weeks. Some of this I still practice, and some I do not.

Monday

Get to the office early Monday morning. Begin praying and searching the Scriptures for the passage you are going to deliver. I am writing this section on a Monday afternoon. I was up at 5:00 a.m., and after my morning routine, I was at my desk writing my sermon by 7:30 a.m. If Monday is typically a day off, you can trade for another day. Get into your desk chair and begin diving into the text you will use. Don't answer a call, check your emails, or go to the bathroom (just kidding) until the skeleton of your outline is on paper. Then outline the text.

Allow me to repeat this: outline the text. You need an outline even if you are going word-by-word through some verses. An outline keeps you grounded and ensures you have an organized frame of thought as you speak. Get to know what the text is saying and where you are going with it. I want my sermon to be 75–85 percent done before I go home on Monday evening. If you're abducted by aliens on Monday evening and dropped back off on Saturday night, you still should be able to preach the sermon. This type of prep will completely change your week, mental stability, stress levels, and especially the upcoming weekend.

Tuesday

On Tuesday, bring your sermon back out. Take a couple of hours to finalize all you can. You might not have your intro or conclusion finalized yet, and that is fine. You might still need an illustration or two, but overall, your sermon should be mostly set.

The rest of the week, you can read, research, and listen to other sermons on your text or topic. Become an expert in what you will be addressing. On Sunday, you will give a TED Talk on the text that the listeners will love.

Wednesday

If you preach for a mid-week service, devote Wednesday to that service. I might have one meeting on Wednesday, but most of the day is dedicated to morning office work and diving into the text or topic I will be speaking on that night. Wednesday nights are a struggle for our teens and adults. They deserve to hear the best to get them through the rest of the week. Most of them will appreciate the extra work you put into the slides, illustrations, and stories to help them pay attention and keep their eyelids from closing.

Thursday

Thursday afternoon, create your slides, handouts, or any other accessory you bring to the table. Put a PowerPoint presentation together that does not take away from the text but gives your audience something to see and learn from. Don't panic over transitions and backgrounds. When your church people watch Sunday Night Football after the service, they won't be talking or thinking about your transitions at halftime. I do hope they're thinking about your sermon though. Use as much Scripture as possible. Looking at Scripture for periods of time could be the most valuable resource they take away from the service.

I have found that a simple black background with white letters or vice versa is most effective for a slide presentation. You want the people to be able to see it. You don't want your audience more interested in your pictures than the Scriptures. And if it blends with the background or the font is too small, they will be more consumed with what they can't see than what you say. They need to hear and see what is being conveyed through the text.

Friday and the Weekend

On Friday and Saturday, forget about your sermon. Enjoy your family and college football. Play golf. Read. Swim. Go to the beach. Rest, and make sure you feel on top of your game when Sunday comes. Friday and Saturday play a major role in Sunday's sermon delivery. Your mind and body need to be 100 percent when Sunday arrives. The running community calls this tapering. You taper before a race to allow your body to be ready to go on race day. The same is true for preaching on Sunday.

I encourage you to think through your sermon on Saturday evenings. I like to do this in my office or even in the auditorium. I also know guys who will have their sermons out in front of them on Saturday evenings while looking through their church directory. I have heard Alistair Begg say that he reads over his sermon before he falls asleep on Saturday nights.

Sunday

Get up early on Sunday morning and go to the church or another spot where you can preach through your sermon. That will ensure that you are comfortable with it and your slides. Make any adjustments needed, and then pray over it. Even if you preach from an iPad, print it off and pray over it. Some of my greatest sermon illustrations and applications came while praying over my sermon.

Go into the pulpit knowing these are God's people, words, and work. You are simply a vessel being used by God to exercise the gifts He's given you where He's called you to do it. His Word will not return void. If you are faithful in delivery, He will do with it as He pleases. The results are a work of God. Don't second-guess yourself when you finish or base its effectiveness on the people's responses. I know one pastor who calls several people on Sunday afternoon and Monday to find confirmation and approval for his sermon. Get up, give the Word, sit down, and let the Spirit do His work.

There should be nothing more satisfying than knowing you did your best. By doing that, you can walk away Sunday with no regrets, knowing you have fulfilled your calling as a faithful servant.

TIME TO REFLECT

1. Think back on a sermon that you put off studying for. Think of a sermon you had to prepare with minimal time, but it was not your fault. Which one went better? Why?
2. What do you see as the greatest hindrance to keeping you from setting up your schedule like this on the weeks you preach?
3. How would your preaching change if you followed this schedule for sermon preparation?

Art of Purity

Things were booming in my friend Wade's youth ministry. He was enjoying life and loving the ministry. Wade was busy, but considering the way God was blessing, he knew it was okay. After all, his wife and children would always be there, but he only had this one shot to become a standout in his circle. His wife, Jamie, loved seeing her husband succeed from a distance and hated that she couldn't be involved in ministry as much as she wanted. But with a new baby and a two-year-old, there was just no way for her to be very involved. At least Wade had some good helpers from the church assisting him on Wednesdays and during activities. Diane and her husband volunteered to start working with Wade soon after he arrived. They were wonderful, and the two couples quickly formed a bond. With Wade's wife being home a lot and Diane's husband putting in more hours than normal at work, there were more and more opportunities for Wade to have "work" conversations with Diane.

Diane's husband attended youth outings with her when he could, but it was Diane who did most of the work and was always there to lend a helping hand. Wade and Diane were alone at church quite often once the teens went home. As they talked, their hearts quickly joined when it came to philosophy and ministry. As time went on, these quiet conversations went from being work-related to casual to much more intimate. They found themselves almost rushing the teens out so they could enjoy the conversations they craved. Wade would be the first to admit that Diane was special. Wade's wife was a great mom, but she seemed more into things at home, whereas Diane seemed more focused on the things of God. It was not long until these spiritual talks became sexual, and when the affair became public, they were never able to again do the ministry they so desperately loved doing together. You have heard this scenario many times and possibly watched this play out in your church. I hate it.

We are living in a day when Christian men and women are regularly falling prey to sexual temptation. I feel like I am past the point of being shocked when I hear about another sexual failure in a ministry. The younger guys who read, watch, and look to these men as mentors and spiritual leaders are continually crushed by their heroes' sins. When someone falls, the next generation begins to wonder if there is any hope. They begin to question everything they have been taught. They wonder if it is even possible to live for Christ. Their young minds begin to believe that all leaders are frauds and failures.

Before going any further, let me say this: sex has no sense. What I mean is that you can't justify this stuff. You can't rationalize it. There is no real way to make sense of it when you hear of another pastor leaving his wife or church for sexual pleasure. We can blame porn, lack of accountability, never being saved, sexual abuse as a child, or whatever. The bottom line is that in most cases, we will never know.

I have tried to go back and analyze every conversation Wade and I had together. We started preaching together when we were both 16. My wife and I have tried to pick apart their marriage to see where they went wrong. There was nothing to find. Wade let his guard down, Satan capitalized on it, and he ruined his ministry, life, and future along with losing the ones he loved most—his wife and children.

I am afraid it is only going to get worse. It's true that our sinful nature is no different than it was 100 years ago, and people were committing adultery then too. But the strange woman of Proverbs had to be found. Men were risking a lot just trying to find her. Now she is in your home, car, and workplace, and even in bed with you and your wife. A hundred years ago, there was no way to send inappropriate pictures. Once you graduated from high school and moved away, that was it. That's not true anymore. With a swipe of a finger, we can engage in, set up, and make happen anything we desire. With modern AI technology, we can even make it happen without consent. I do not envy the younger generation. It is no longer a magazine a boy stole from the store or an uncle left in the barn. It is much more real, available, and pervasive.

Years ago, I read in a Christian magazine an article titled "Standing in the Rain." It was about a man who saw a female church member standing on the side of the road in the rain, and instead of giving her a ride, he gave her his car and went out in the rain. As a young man, I found that strange and extreme. His point was that he could not risk having that woman seen in the car with him.

Today it is different. Since the writing of that article, things have changed drastically. If the woman was stuck in the rain today, she would call an Uber. Instead of purchasing pornography, we can stream it on Netflix. If we need a place to hook up, we can rent an Airbnb with a garage to hide the car. Today, a woman doesn't need to be in our car because she is in our contacts. We can access who we want when we want. We can send an invisible text or a secret message. We can ensure the inappropriate picture is deleted in 10 seconds and prevent screenshots from being taken. We can cover our backs in so many ways that it is almost impossible to get caught.

Satan knows that if he can destroy you and eventually your family, he has won. Your church will never trust you again. Your wife will be living in fear and suspicion for years. Your children will always be torn between mom and dad. The name of Christ will be scorned in your community and beyond. I once would hear of this situation and think, *I could never do that to my wife or children*. Many of you have thought the same thing.

Recently, I heard some couples justify their actions with one word: *consent*. It was okay for them to mess around with others because their spouse knew about it. As long as they were okay with it, it was perfectly justifiable.

I know we can pick that apart, but listen, if I am staying sexually solo for my wife, I could still succumb to temptation. I do not stay in a monogamous relationship because of my wife. I do so because that is what God says I should do. We should not be asking ourselves, "How could I do that to my wife?" We should ask, "How could I ever do that to Christ?"

We naturally think, *If I loved my wife and kids more, I wouldn't be falling into this stuff.* There will be days you won't love your spouse very much. There will be a day when somebody who is more attractive than your spouse will come into your life—a person with a great sense of humor, dreamy eyes, deep compassion, and seems to understand you better than your spouse does. If you had to find a soul mate, this would be the one. They just understand you. They *do* get you. Satan has seen to it that they do.

Prevention is not loving your spouse more; it is falling in love with Jesus. You need such a love for Jesus that you would never be tempted to sin against Him. You need such a love for Jesus that you would never dream of sinning against the One who died for your sin. You need such a love to do work for His Kingdom that you wouldn't dream of doing anything that would disqualify you.

If I am truly where I need to be with Christ, I should have a very difficult time walking across the street after my devotions and jumping in bed with my neighbor. I should be sweating bullets while texting inappropriate content just before I preach the Word. I should never want to go from my computer study program to porn on the same computer.

Christ must be real in our lives. We must desire Him and a relationship with Him more than anyone or anything else. We should be praying without ceasing. We should be singing praises to Him continually. We should be bringing every thought into captivity to be monitored by Christ.

We can't afford to play games in our spiritual lives. We cannot be messing around and expecting God to be okay with it. It is time to take control and live a life where God is glorified, which was not the case for Ravi Zacharias.

So, how can we ensure a pure life? How can we know when the temptation comes (and it will)? Will we run or be righteous?

Again, there is no way to have all the answers. You are young. You're full of energy. Your life is exciting. You are a dynamic speaker. You know how to dress and look good. Satan sees all of this and will make sure he uses it to his advantage. But let me encourage with a few personal warnings.

Personal Warnings

1. **Be aware of your surroundings.** If it has not happened yet, it will. Satan knows when you are tired. He knows when you are alone. He knows when you and your spouse are at odds. There will be multiple occasions where the devil will put you in a position where it will be very easy for you to fall. I remember sitting in the lobby of a Hilton hotel when a very attractive woman sat down beside me so closely that she had to place her briefcase on the other side of her. As she started the conversation, it was evident she was looking for more than a conversation about the weather. Before you begin fantasizing about this, fast forward 24 hours when you must try to forget what you did while walking in and hugging your wife and kids, praying they never find out.
2. **Prepare for battle.** You need to understand that there will always be a battle. I don't care whether you have

perfect hair or no hair. I don't care whether you have a dad bod or are jacked. There will always be a battle with the idea of sexuality. It may be going on right in front of you or on your phone.

The algorithms of Instagram and Facebook are no accident. They know where you go. Your flirting is flooding your phone with garbage. You are being hunted. But it's time to turn the tide. It's time to stop being the hunted and be the hunter. It's time for you to be the warrior. It's time for you to stand against this stuff. It's time for you to not allow Instagram, Facebook, or anything else to win. It's time for you to take a stand and flip the script.

Kill it! Paul says to kill it—to mortify the deeds of the flesh. Listen! Be the hunter! Stop getting caught in these traps.

Several years ago, I was sitting in a golf cart with an older believer from my church. He told me this: "Treg, I'm 73 years old. And let me tell you, when it comes to sexual temptation, it doesn't get any easier." Listen, men! He was right.

Yes, it's a battle. But yes, there is hope, and you are the generation to overcome this. You are the generation that people have looked at for years and said, "You know, there is potential in these men." You no longer have to be the hunted. You have the ability and power to become the hunter. It's time for you to kill the algorithm. It is time to prove to social media that you no longer need it. It's time for you to become the warrior.

3. **Set boundaries.** Parents and pastors often ask me, "What are the best things I can use to filter my phone or my kid's phone?" There are many programs and apps that are great, but they only go so far. You can take all the alcohol out of the home of an alcoholic, but they can still find their fix just about anywhere.

   To avoid temptation, strict Muslims do not allow women into their mosques. Books are circulated among these Muslim men that warn about a woman's perfume and how it lures you in as a temptation to the flesh. But does that change the evil heart from being corrupted inside? No. These are some of the same mosque members who gang rape women and children in an act of Holy Jihad.

   Forts are great, but those living within them must be prepared for battle. What must happen in order to become a warrior? What should you do to become the hunter and stop being the hunted? You have to have a change of heart.

Scriptural Warnings

I've shared with you some personal examples. Now let's look at some Scriptural examples.

1. **Abraham.** Abraham the adulterer, Abraham and his sister wives—that is not how the Bible describes Abraham. That's what makes this difficult. We don't see him referred to as Abe the adulterer, and we don't sing, "Father Abraham had many wives." What we do find is Abraham the friend of God. Did God justify Abraham's actions? Was God okay with Abraham sleeping with his servant? What justification did he have?

- It was acceptable regarding current culture and practice. Ancient law said if you could not have an heir through your wife, you could have one through your servant.
- It was consensual. Not only was it culturally acceptable, but it was consensual. It was Sarah's idea. Hagar was not resisting either. It ensured that her seed would continue with the blessing of a wealthy father. This was a great thing for her, and she looked on it as something special. Humanly speaking, this was a win-win in Abraham's book. Or was it?

In the eyes of God, this was a huge failure in Abraham's life and concerning his faith, which later God had to test. There were also major consequences to pay. His wife was unhappy and jealous, and we are still dealing today with the issues between these two brothers.

God's plan is the perfect plan. I don't care whether you or your wife is okay with it. I don't care whether your spouse hasn't touched you in months or you think they are cheating on you. You are never justified to be sexually active outside of your marriage.

Abraham should have stepped up and said no. He knew God's plan and promise to Sarah. He knew the plan was not with Hagar. That is not what God promised or the plan He had established. When David committed adultery, he said to God, "Against you and you only have I sinned." David got it.

You must get it. Even after repentance and forgiveness, there will be consequences, not just tomorrow or when you get caught, but for generations to come.

2. **Judah.** How about Judah? The passage in Genesis about Judah and the passage that deals with David and Bathsheba are two of my least favorite in the Bible. I could have skipped over them in my yearly Bible reading. Genesis 38 is a crazy passage. I can't explain it all, and I do not want to, but we can draw some important conclusions from it.
   - Never justify a one-night stand. *No one will know. She has no idea who I am, and we won't continue this more than just tonight. It doesn't matter. After tonight, we'll go on with our lives. No one will ever know.*

     It doesn't work that way. In this story, Tamar had the seal and the staff, and she could call out Judah later on. Do you remember the story? We might not have a seal and staff today, but we have social media and a cell phone.

     You have a phone number and messenger. Your name is all over the Internet, and there's no way to hide those things anymore. One day after a one-night stand, you'll get a message in private mode. This woman has somehow found you without even knowing your name. And now there is no way to make this disappear. There's nowhere to hide.
   - Be very careful when traveling alone. If possible, never travel alone. Tamar knew Judah was alone. He was doing his own thing. No one was around. Why not take advantage of this business trip? Again, had Judah gotten a hotel room with a double bed for him and his assistant and not the king-size bed, I wouldn't have to skip chapter 38.

Traveling alone is sometimes unavoidable. But I'm telling you, men and women, it's very, very difficult. It is nearly impossible to sneak into somebody else's bedroom or sneak somebody else into your bedroom when you're sharing that room with a friend, another pastor, or an intern. I'm not saying it hasn't happened, but I'm telling you that Ravi Zacharias, Bill Hybels, Bob Coy, Jack Hyles, and his son-in-law Jack Schaap didn't have somebody with them. But God was there, and He made sure their sins found them out.

3. **Amnon.** "Amnon had a friend" (2 Sam. 13:3). Amnon had a lot of things, and a walk with God was not one of them. He allowed his heart to passionately seek, dream about, and dwell on another woman. Jesus makes it clear that as a man thinks in his heart, so he is, and Amnon proves it.

Amnon had already committed fornication with this woman in his heart. Amnon wasn't married, but even still, he was obligated to keep his heart and mind pure. If you are married, this is an even greater issue. You could easily commit adultery in your heart regularly. It might be someone at the coffee shop, a coworker, or a neighbor. It might be some woman you don't even know that you're fantasizing about on your phone. It might be the woman at the bookstore.

Stop fantasizing. Listen to what Solomon says about our wandering love. "Rejoice with the wife of thy youth" (Prov. 5:18). And she is the only person you need to think about.

4. **David.** You all know the story. We've heard and preached thousands of applications from this story. Stay busy. Plan your time off. Don't look, and don't go where you can look. Go to battle, and so on. There can be much here, but God's purpose and rebuke to David through Nathan is about being content. In essence, Nathan is saying, "David, you have beautiful wives. Why are you not content with what you have?" Contentment is the key. God wants you to be content with your wife, always with your wife.

Your wife might not look like a beautiful model, but how many children has that model given birth to? What would her body look like if she had four kids by now? Men, this is the beauty of God's creation. Those are marks of triumph. Your wife endured an ultra-marathon to bring children into this world. Your family should be something you glory in. Your marriage should be something you rejoice in and not be tempted to go to somebody else. Be content. God wants you to be content with the wife He has given you.

Solomon goes on to say, "Drink waters out of thine own cistern" (Prov. 5:15). Stop trying to find sexual pleasure from someone else. Solomon tells his son to be content, to be satisfied with the wife of his youth. He said that to ensure it's only his kids running in the streets.

I do not envy any of you right now. Many of the men you have read, looked up to, and desired to emulate in your life have fallen. Ask God to give you a desire in your heart to stop being the hunted, to stop running, cowering, and falling. You are much like a deer that hears the gunfire in the woods and cowers. You're cowering under sexual attack. It's time to fight. It's time to ask the Lord to help you to fight.

I want to see a generation of young men come up in the ministry where I rarely hear of anyone falling into sexual temptation or splitting up families or leaving their homes. Are any of you losing your ministries over sin? God has made a way to escape. God has given you the power to say enough is enough and turn off your phone. Don't go to it anymore. Delete the app. Take it off your phone and stop providing a way. Ask God to give you a heart and a desire that loves Him more.

It's not a one-time fight. This is a battle you all are enlisted in. This is something that will continue for the rest of your lives. Does it get easier at times? Yes. But that does not mean your weaknesses will go away.

Be encouraged by what else Solomon says. "Let thy fountain be blessed: and rejoice with the wife of thy youth. Let her be as the loving hind and pleasant roe. Let her breasts satisfy thee at all times; and be thou ravished always with her love. And why wilt thou, my son, be ravished with a strange woman, and embrace the bosom of a stranger?" (Prov. 15:18–20).

Make these words your own, and become a warrior for purity, for your marriage, and for your home. Then instill a warrior spirit into the next generation after you.

TIME TO REFLECT

1. What drastic measures would you have to take right now to keep yourself sexually pure in thought and deed?
2. What is keeping you from following your advice in the answer above?
3. Who do you know who has fallen into sexual sin? How did it affect you? What did you learn from it? What are some steps you could take that they didn't to help protect you from the same fate?

Art of Suffering

This is a chapter I would love to omit or have someone else write. It is also a chapter I feel I have the most experience in. Suffering is something many of us know and the rest will find out. Suffering comes in a variety of ways, forms, waves, and seasons. I've known men who have gone through things in ministry that I could not even imagine I have also had men tell me the same about my seasons of suffering. Let's look closely at the background and examples of suffering. And there will be warning signals of where suffering can take a minister if it's not dealt with properly.

Burnout

Ministry stinks! You possibly have said this to yourself or others over the years. It is hard. It is a burden. There are sleepless nights and very long days. It is not a business where you are concerned only with the bottom line or the dollar. It is a concern that runs deep as you share with people in their every tear, joy, and sorrow. You celebrate with them when their baby is born and mourn with them when their loved ones pass away. You hunt, run, and eat with them and will very possibly stand over them while you preach at their funeral. When they lose a family member, you feel as though you have lost a family member. You love these sheep and have given everything for them.

The hurt comes due to the sheep's ability to quickly forget. As soon as you do something they don't like, you are their greatest enemy and foe. It is amazing how quickly a friend can turn their back on you and walk away as if you never cared.

As if this isn't bad enough, the stress of the job also brings personal pain and suffering. There are days when you should be home but feel you need to be in the office. There are days when you would love to be playing ball with the kids, but you feel you need to be out making a visit. You want to take the evening for your family, but as soon as you see who is calling, you know you must answer the phone. When you finally hang up, your kids are in bed, and your wife is asleep on the couch.

You are on medicine for your heartburn. Your stomach is always messed up with irritable bowel syndrome (IBS) issues. There has been at least one time, if not twice, when you thought you were having a heart attack. Your blood pressure is not where it should be, and you've put on 20 pounds since your college days. Your doctor has told you to slow down and calm down, but you don't see that as a possibility. You pray and ask God for grace, but it doesn't stop the health issues. If this sounds familiar, beware. You are on the verge of burning out.

In 2001 when Carrie and I were engaged, she bought her first car. It was a white 1996 Honda Accord. It was a great investment, and we knew it would last her for many years to come, at least we thought it would. On a trip to Ohio to see me, Carrie noticed that two men in a car were following her. She was scared to stop, so she drove straight to my house. Two hundred miles later, that Honda engine was making some strange noises. At first it seemed okay, but she only got about 20,000 more miles out of it before it blew up. The low oil light had been on since her trip to Ohio. Running that motor with no oil was a very costly mistake. It only cost her a car, but for many it has cost them their lives. We were not made to run on empty.

Suicide

On September 9, 2019, California megachurch pastor and author Jarrid Wilson, who frequently spoke out on the issues of mental health and his struggles with depression, committed suicide at the age of 30.

Pastor and author Darrin Patrick died on May 7, 2020, just outside of St. Louis. The cause of death was a self-inflicted gunshot wound. He was 49.

Megachurch pastor Andrew Stoecklein, age 30, was at work inside the Inland Hills Church his father founded in Chino, California, when he committed suicide on Friday, August 24, 2018.

Marilane Carter, 36-year-olf mother of three young children and wife of a Baptist pastor, left her home in Overland Park, Kansas, in July 2020. Her body was found in August inside her car in an empty storage container on private property. She had committed suicide.

Suffering and depression can take over our minds, causing us to nearly drown in the depths of despair. When sickness, setbacks, suffering, and pain come, it is challenging to keep pressing forward. You may not have said it verbally, but mentally you may have been at a point when you felt there was only one way out.

Physical

Our bodies were not created to handle stress. I am convinced it is a major contributor to many of the health issues that pastors face. When I became the pastor of Faith Baptist Church in Morgantown, I told my family that we would not be taking any vacations because I needed to be the pastor of Faith every Sunday for the next year. The problem was that it went on to the next year as well. Sixteen months later, I took a four-week, unplanned sabbatical beginning on September 17, 2023, at approximately 7:40 p.m., when I was rushed to the hospital by way of ambulance. The paramedics put two pads on my chest, and one paramedic sat beside me holding the paddles to bring me back to life if necessary. I was having a heart attack, a massive heart attack.

My EKG was throwing what is called tombstones. They're called that because they look like tombstones but also because medical professionals know their patient will be under a tombstone shortly. I was dying due to a 100 percent blockage in my left ventricle, also known as the widow-maker. I had a four percent chance of survival. Was it my lifestyle or diet that caused this? It had been 10 days since I finished in the top 10 of the Morgantown marathon. I had a "green machine" smoothie for lunch. It was not my lifestyle; it was my vocation. Satan attacked, and God allowed me to endure that suffering.

Let's go back to Super Bowl Sunday in 2019. I was still in the hospital, recovering from surgery on my colon. I had a serious infection due to Crohn's disease, and it required emergency surgery. I told my wife to go home and clean up. I was going to rest and watch the football game. It was just before 6:00 p.m. when things started to go wrong. I felt my heart rate go up, and I became extremely weak. I called for my nurse, who informed me I had a fever of 104° Fahrenheit, and my heart rate was 160. The medical staff ran blood quickly through the lab and informed me I was septic, and they were transporting me to the ICU.

Why does God allow His servants to suffer like this in His service? How do the lost and heathen prosper and seem to have little to no illnesses, yet we as God's servants endure so much? I genuinely believe that if you are doing what God wants and what Satan does not, you will be attacked. Satan will do everything in his power to stop you. It was Satan who attacked Job. It was Satan who desired to sift the disciples. It was Satan who went after Jesus. It was one of Satan's minions who was battling Paul. Why couldn't it be Satan who is opposing us?

Why does God allow this to happen? Couldn't we serve God to a greater extent and ability without a physical ailment? Wouldn't I be more effective in the office or on the mission field if I didn't always have to be looking for a restroom? Possibly. Or maybe my ministry wouldn't be nearly as effective as it currently is had I not been given this thorn in the flesh. Maybe your ministry also requires such suffering.

Below are seven ways I've seen God use suffering in my personal life and in the lives of others.

Reasons for Suffering

1. **To break us.** God must break us to make us into vessels for His glory. The only way for the jar of clay to shine forth the light within is to be broken. Paul's body was broken over and over. He says of those experiences, "I bear in my body the marks of the Lord Jesus" (Gal. 6:17).
2. **To bring comfort to others.** Time after time, God has given me a platform to share my story with others and encourage them in their sickness and even depression. The way we can extend comfort and encouragement is magnified when the recipient knows we are speaking from experience. It would be wonderful if there were another way for me to relate to others who struggle with Crohn's disease or heart disease, but unfortunately, there is not.
3. **To bring Him glory.** This phrase has become a symbol of Christianity in many ways. "He is greater than I" makes for great shirts and stickers, but the process of that journey is one many might not be willing to sign up for. John the Baptist lost the few followers he had to Jesus. He was thrown into prison and not rescued by Jesus. His beliefs eventually cost him his life. In the book *12 Faithful Men: Portraits of Courageous Endurance in Pastoral Ministry*, it says, "Many of us fervently and repeatedly pray for removal from our circumstances, but God will not change them due to a larger and infinitely more glorious plan that you do not see—namely, your decreasing and his increasing. And God will give you something even greater than the removal of the thorn; he will use all his strength to shine through your brokenness."

4. **God wants more fruit.** Christ loves it when we produce and generate fruit (Gal. 5:22–23) for His Kingdom. But the Lord wants more. God has on His agenda to take us from good to great. Notice the progression in John 15:2. We go from bearing fruit to bearing more fruit. Then we are asked to bear *much fruit*. The only way for this to happen is by pruning (John 15:5). Fruit-producing people require pruning.

   Not everything God removes is bad, but it may not be right for us at the time. So, God must take it away. God has taken my health and strength away from me countless times. I have been robbed of all my dignity and pride numerous times while I was in a hospital. It is frustrating and challenging, but we must trust that He knows what is best for us.

5. **To teach us obedience.** Christ learned obedience. How is that even possible? Through suffering, Christ became obedient unto death (Phil. 2:8). Through suffering, Christ "learned" and teaches us to trust. It is a trusting obedience. It is a confidence that not my will, but God's will is best. The only way for us as God's servants to learn this obedience is through suffering. The only way I can truly trust Him is when He slays me (Job 13:15).

6. **To conform us to Christ's image.** The ultimate goal for every believer is to be Christ-like. We all are very familiar with Romans 8:28, but I hope we are as equally familiar with Romans 8:29. Paul says, all things (even seasons of suffering) work together for good because we are on a mission "to be conformed to the image of his Son." Christ is

the resilient Lion of Judah on the inside and the Lamb of God on the outside. Suffering will humble us but at the same time make us stronger in Him.
7. **To help us focus on eternity.** Often, a change in perspective is all we need. Paul would have never made it had his eyes been focused on his present circumstances (2 Cor. 4:1, 16). His perspective on the eternal took his "despaired even of life" scenario (2 Cor. 1:8) to a momentary "light affliction" (2 Cor. 4:17). His heart's desire was to be with Christ, but he knew his work on earth was not done.

Paul could have told us about the wonders of heaven in 2 Corinthians 12, but he shared with us something he felt was far greater. He said God did not want him to share about heaven but about suffering, which is what Paul did. R. Kent Hughes says in his book *2 Corinthians: Power in Weakness*, "Nowhere is Paul's heart so torn and exposed as in this letter." Paul is discouraged and having a very difficult time facing reality. He begins this letter with a Jewish prayer of praise but then takes a drastic turn to dive right into the description of the God he desperately needs.

The Father of mercies and God of all comfort (2 Cor. 1:3) was who Paul was clinging to in this desperate situation. He said that he and Timothy "had no rest, but we were troubled on every side—without were fightings, within were fears" (2 Cor. 7:5).

The God of compassion and comfort is a God like no other. He is our comfort. He looks upon us with compassion. He is not sitting in heaven looking for reasons to judge us or make our lives miserable. His mood does not change like the gods of other religions, but this does not mean that suffering will be eliminated from our lives. It is the complete opposite at times. Even if you have faced difficulties before, that won't be the last time you face them, and you don't want it to be. This is where true growth and strength lie.

The Origin of Suffering

So where does this suffering come from? In Job, it seems like it comes from Satan. Is Satan the one who causes our suffering? When hardships come and bad things happen to good people, we tend to categorize those events in one of two categories—circumstances or Satan. How about the Bubonic plague, SIDS, hurricanes, car troubles, a broken leg, missionaries captured and held for ransom or even killed? Surely this is all of Satan, right? Yes.

God Is Sovereign

Job was troubled by Satan. Jesus told Peter that Satan desired to have him to sift him. Paul was given a messenger of Satan to torment and harass him. Satan seems like the guilty party here. I am convinced that even my heart attack and Crohn's disease could very possibly have been brought on by Satan. But as theologian R. C. Sproul once said, "Satan can do only what the sovereign God allows him to do."

Scripture Is Sufficient

There is nothing that has transpired in my life, even delivered by Satan, that God has not allowed. Before anything can happen to us, it must go through God's throne. This alone should bring us comfort, as should the Word of God, our source of strength and hope. In my darkest days, I wrote in my Job journal Bible. That was in 2019, and I still haven't gone back to read it. Those days were so long and painful that I have no desire to relive them. But God's Word was my comfort. Even to this day I tear up when I hear Job 13:15, "Though he slay me." God used that verse to get me through those dark days.

Grace Is Sufficient

God takes us through or allows Satan to take us through suffering to trust Him fully. Sometimes God does this by putting us in a place of total reliance. It is the only way we stop trusting in ourselves. This is where God wants us. He must be the One to receive the glory. When we find ourselves fully relying on Him, we are giving Him the glory He deserves.

When we rely on Him, He chooses to send the rescue. Paul says in 2 Corinthians 1:10 that God has, does, and will deliver us. God sometimes delivers by practical means. He delivered me from death but allowed the surgeon to put a stent in my left ventricle. God delivered Paul by allowing pieces of the broken ship to pass by. He delivers by providential means. When I made my appointments with Cleveland Clinic, little did I know that the two doctors who had an opening in their schedule were world-renowned Crohn's and colorectal specialists. God did.

Last but not least, God uses prayer. In Philippians 1:19, Paul says, "For I know that this shall turn to my salvation through your prayer, and the supply of the Spirit of Jesus Christ." God rescues us through the prayers of the saints.

Personal Examples

You still might be thinking, "I don't get it. It doesn't seem fair." I know, but let's see how God has used suffering in men of God throughout church history.

Paul

Had the Apostle Paul not been imprisoned, we would not have a vital and beloved section in our Bibles—the prison epistles.

John Bunyan

Had John Bunyan not been imprisoned for preaching the gospel in England, many of us would have never been inspired by *Pilgrim's Progress*.

Charles Simeon

Without the difficulties and hardships from the congregation at Holy Trinity Church, we would be missing out on Charles Simeon, a man who should inspire us greatly. Upset that the bishop had called Simeon as their pastor, the church hired their own pastor and paid him double what Charles was receiving. That forced Charles to move his service to Sunday afternoons. To stop this, the members locked their rented pews and would not allow any afternoon attendees to sit in them. As a result, all who attended had to sit in the aisle on benches that Simeon rented. He was locked out of his church on Sunday nights to prevent him from holding evening services. He was attacked by members on various occasions. He exited different doors on Sunday afternoons to escape from being beaten. He was greeted with rotten eggs after leaving church one Sunday. On various afternoons, attendees would be stoned and harassed.

Due to Charles' faithfulness, we have reaped the benefits of various college groups such as InterVarsity and others around the world. These groups in return produced men such as John Stott and Kent Hughes.

William Carey

William Carey is known as the father of modern missions. This would not be the case without the suffering he endured. When he was well-established in his pioneer missionary work in India, his supporters in England sent a printing press to assist him. Soon, he was turning out portions of the Bible for distribution. Carey had spent many years learning the language to produce the Scriptures in the local dialect. He had also prepared dictionaries and grammars for his successors to use.

On March 11, 1812, Carey was teaching in a Bible college when a fire broke out in the printing room. Despite many hours of intense efforts to fight the fire, the locals couldn't stop the building from burning to the ground. Carey's entire library, his completed Sanskrit dictionary, part of his Bengal dictionary, two grammar books, and 10 translations of the Bible were lost. Gone also were the typesets for printing in 14 languages. The vast quantities of English paper, priceless dictionaries, deeds, and account books were gone as well.

When Carey returned to Serampore and surveyed the scene, he wept and later wrote in his journal, "In one short evening, the labors of years are consumed. How unsearchable are the ways of God? I had lately brought some things to the utmost perfection of which they seemed capable and contemplated the missionary establishment with perhaps too much self-congratulation. The Lord has laid me low, that I may look more simply to him."

Although he was heartbroken, he did not take much time to mourn. With great resilience, Carey went on to write, "The loss is heavy, but as traveling a road the second time is usually done with greater ease than the first time, so I trust the work will lose nothing of real value. We are not discouraged; indeed, the work has already begun again in every language. We are cast down but not in despair."

Carey resolved to trust God that a better printing press and more scholarly translations would come from the embers of that fire. Little did he know that the fire would bring him and his work to the attention of people all over Europe, America, and India. In just 50 days, from England and Scotland alone, about £10,000 was raised for rebuilding Carey's publishing enterprise. So much money was coming in that Andrew Fuller, Carey's friend and a leader of his mission in England, told his committee when he returned from a fundraising trip, "We must stop the contributions."

Many volunteers came to India to help as well. By 1832, Carey had rebuilt and expanded printing operations and published complete Bibles or portions of the Bible in 44 languages and dialects. "Though he slay me, yet will I trust him" (Job 13:15).

TIME TO REFLECT

1. Looking back on your life, how has God used tragedy to help make you into a trophy for His grace?
2. Who are some people you know who God is greatly using because of suffering? How has God done that?
3. Take time to study the life of Job, Bunyan, Simeon, or Carey. You will find that their blessings far outweighed their sufferings in the end.

Art of Knowing What's Next

What's next is a question many of you probably ask yourself on a regular basis. You find yourself daydreaming at times about working for or with certain pastors or ministries. You long for the day when God opens the door for you to head elsewhere. Others reading this might be praying that God leaves you right where you are. You have no desire to leave, and you love serving with your pastor and church. I love that. Regardless, I do feel that the necessary and practical steps mentioned in this chapter will be of help to you even if you are settled in for the long haul.

What is next is fun to dream about but a reality you most likely will not be made aware of until it is time. God does not lay out road maps of our future for us. The future would scare us to death, and too many of us would be like Jonah and run. I would have. Carrie and I were friends in college and nothing more. If God had told me I would marry her at the age of 20, I would have laughed. Two years after high school graduation, we were married in Morgantown, West Virginia. If God would have said that 12 years later, I would pastor this church, I would have purchased a ticket to Tarshish. The fact is that we don't know the mind of God. As a senior in college, if God had told me I had 16 years ahead of me as an assistant, I would have corrected Him.

God's ways are not our ways. His thoughts are not our thoughts. Looking back, it is plain to see that His hand was guiding me. I trust you can say the same. So, if God is the guide and sovereign in leading us, what's next?

Necessary Steps

To be ready for what's next you must be:

1. **Content where you are.** I cannot emphasize this enough. Contentment is crucial when it comes to what is next. I am sure there were times when Esther would have loved to be anywhere other than where God had her. I am sure there were days in Cyprus that Barnabas missed his days on the road with Paul. Don't get me wrong. Cyprus is beautiful, but I'm sure there were times when Barnabas longed to see God do the extraordinary again.

    We must be content in whatever state we're in, wherever God has you, whatever the situation looks like. You cannot show disgust with God about your current status and expect Him to give you what you want. It just doesn't work that way. God has put you exactly where you need to be. Believe it or not, you are in the perfect place.

2. **Serving and working where you are.** Serving in your current ministry might not be the best right now. I know there are days when you wish you were anywhere other than where you currently are. I know the agony of going

through the motions. You look out your window and think about all the other ministries or places you could be and how much good you could be doing elsewhere. Be careful. This is a huge problem. When I get into this state of mind, I completely miss how valuable I could be where God currently has me. You have no idea how God can use you because your eyes are continually looking elsewhere.

I'm not saying that God doesn't have somewhere else for you to go, but I am saying that you need to make the most of where you are. God has a purpose and a reason for leaving you there. He is in complete control of all the resources you have in your current ministry.

As I look back on my previous ministries and some of my journal entries, I see there were days when I asked God how much longer I had to be here. There were other days that I wrote about how God was using me here. It was a year and a half before God decided to move me on. But as I look back on that year and a half, God took me through a lot but also taught me a lot that I needed to learn to prepare me for what was to come.

Don't give up. God is working in and through you, despite what you think. Take a step back, get your eyes off the negative, and look at the positive that is happening. When God moved me on from one of my ministries, I received a message on social media from a young person in my youth group. He said that he understood God wanted me to move on but still felt hurt that I would go.

Why would he say that? I didn't realize it at the time, but God was using me in the life of this young man. Looking back, I wish I would have spent more time with him. Obviously, it was enough to make an impact, but I know I could have done more. I was maybe too busy thinking about what was next and not focusing on the present.

The words of Martin Luther King Jr. should inspire us. He said, "If a man is called to be a street sweeper, he should sweep streets even as Michelangelo painted, or Beethoven composed music or Shakespeare wrote poetry. He should sweep streets so well that all hosts of heaven and earth will pause to say: Here lives a great street sweeper who did his job well."

3. **Willing to go.** Jonah was willing to go anywhere but where God was asking him to go. Isaiah, unsure of what was being asked, cried out, "Here am I; send me" (Isa. 6:8).

I have talked to men who serve in the Special Forces. Many of them have a bag packed and ready to go at a moment's notice. When they receive that call to go on a mission, they have no choice in the matter. They must go. In certain cases, they might not even have time to give their loved ones a hug goodbye. Duty calls.

Paul uses the illustration of a soldier when describing Timothy's calling to the ministry. "Thou therefore endure hardness, as a good soldier of Jesus Christ. No man that warreth entangleth himself with the affairs of this life; that he may please him who hath chosen him to be a soldier" (2 Tim. 2:3–4). God is our commanding officer. He gives the orders. We are simply to obey. Timothy's calling was a difficult one. Ephesus was not an easy place to minister. Berea was probably more Timothy's speed. I am sure he felt his gift set and personality were more suited for a smaller city or congregation. But that was not his call to make. Paul encouraged Timothy to stay the course and continue following the orders of his commanding officer.

We don't get to write our orders. Our commanding officer determines where He wants us and what He wants from us. If I were in charge of my own orders, I would be looking out my window now at palm trees, not at 5 inches of snow. But it's not about what I want; it's about what God wants. It's not about geography; it's about people. You could be looking at palm trees, and God might call you to the snowy pines. Go! Do what God wants you to do, even when it doesn't make sense. Always be yielded and available for what God has for you next.

4. **Willing to give up some things.** Bigger and better is not always the modus operandi of the Lord. Naturally, it seems like that's the way it should be, right? If I have been successful in a smaller ministry, surely God has a bigger ministry for me. If I have been faithful and serving God in the area that He has for me on the West Coast, He will move me back to where I want to be on the East Coast, right? Not necessarily. There are times when God calls us to go places that might not be exactly what we've imagined in our minds. You may have to let go of certain things when you go to your next ministry.

You might go from a large youth room to no youth room. You might go from having a large office to having a small office. You might go from having two large soccer fields to no soccer field. You might go from a Mac-only ministry to a Windows ministry (you might reconsider going if that is the case). You might go from a church bus to a 15-passenger van.

You see, these things don't matter when it comes to service. One day, when I stand before the Lord, I'm not going to give an account of the size of my office or how great a backdrop of books I have. I'm going to give an account of the people God has called me to watch over. We should be willing to give up whatever it is that God wants us to give up in order to hear these words: "Well done, good and faithful servant" (Matt. 25:23).

5. **Unenamored with titles.** When assistant pastors look at what's next, they often believe their next ministry will be in the role of a senior pastor. After all, I've been working as an assistant for five years. It only makes sense now that I become a senior pastor. But what if God is not ready for you to step into that role?

I had no desire to be a youth pastor, a college pastor, or even an assistant pastor when I was a senior in college. I wanted to be a lead. Through high school and college, I was captain of sports teams, president of my classes, and normally always found myself in a position of leadership. I enjoyed that and felt that leadership was my gift. I assumed that was how God would use me after college. Oh, how wrong I was! I went from a 22-year-old thinking I needed to be a senior pastor to a 38-year-old finally becoming a senior pastor. It took 16 years for God to put me in that position. Did I need three ministries as an assistant under three pastors over a period of 16 years in order to become a senior pastor? No. I needed more time. God had many things for me to learn so I could be the pastor He needed me to be.

In my first ministry, I learned much about being a pastor and what it meant to serve in that role. In my next ministry, there was a large Christian school. I saw all it took to have a successful Christian school. Coming to Faith and serving under Pastor Bennie Moran, I learned the value of faithfulness and integrity. All of these were lessons I needed to learn in order to become the person, husband, and Father God wanted me to be.

Don't despise vertical steps or what the world would call taking a step back or below where you currently are. I have seen many senior pastors leave their ministries and take positions as assistants. From the outside looking in, this looks like a horrible decision. But from the inside looking out, it was the right decision for their growth and development. God makes no mistakes. Do not let the wisdom of this world determine how you make a decision. The world's wisdom is foolishness for God.

6. **Directed by God.** I truly believe what God has for you next will be directed solely by Him. "The steps of a good man are ordered by the LORD" (Ps. 37:23). It will be something you probably never saw coming. It will be a move God makes that may shock you and probably scare

you even slightly. When that call, email, or conversation happens, you will gulp, take a step back, and ask God if He knows what He's doing.

When I received the phone call about possibly coming to Faith, I was candidating at another ministry. I didn't think serving at Faith would work out. I was pursuing and making plans to go to the other ministry, but God directed my steps to Morgantown, and I am so glad He did.

7. **Aware that what's next will be preceded by a unique desire.** I truly believe God leads us through our righteous desires. Psalm 37:4 says, "Delight thyself also in the LORD, and he shall give thee the desires of thine heart." God implants desires in you to prepare you for what He has. When I was in North Carolina, I began to develop a real love for college students. I would go to the local community college and just hang out in the library one day a week. It started when I met two college students who had a free period. We sat together at a table, which filled up with about 12 of us talking together. Students I didn't know asked me to pray with them before they had to take a test or quiz. I developed a love for working with those college kids.

Little did I know that God would bring me to a college town. I could not have known that a college ministry would be a big part of what I would do and how God would use it to build His church in Morgantown. That was a desire I could not have imagined or acknowledged at the time, but it was there. And when God does that, He is giving you exactly what you want.

God Is Preparing You for What's Next

We must remember that we are exactly where God wants us to be. Perhaps you or the ministry you are in has changed. You could have made a dumb decision and went when you should have stayed. But at this moment, you are where you are, and you need to exercise contentment to the best of your ability. Paul told us he was content in some crazy circumstances as well.

I had a good friend who was a missionary in Zimbabwe. He was home on furlough and taught a class in our church. He spoke on 2 Timothy 2, and it was one of the best lessons I had ever heard on that chapter. Later, I told him he had a unique gift for teaching. He said, "I have always wanted to be a college teacher. I feel very comfortable doing that. But God has called me to Zimbabwe to serve Him there." He was content in Zimbabwe and died serving there. He was a faithful servant to the end, content in his calling.

Practical Steps

After serving in three states and three ministries, and having lived in 12 homes, I've experienced both the right way and the wrong way to prepare for ministry transitions. Allow me to give you some practical advice about preparing for what's next.

1. **Don't hold on to earthly goods.** You can't take it with you. Do not allow yourself to become attached to stuff. If God calls you to move, some of those prized possessions might not make it into the moving truck.
2. **Prepare yourself financially.** You never want to go from one ministry to another and have debt or a financial crisis follow you. Do everything you can in

your current ministry to eliminate any debt you have incurred. I understand that you might be living from income tax return to income tax return, but don't accumulate debt as you await another check from the IRS. Don't accumulate debt as you dream of a raise or how things will one day turn around financially. Finances are a burden, and you don't want to carry that burden from one state to another, from one ministry to another. Set yourself up to be financially free. It could be that when you move, you'll face an unexpected financial situation that you did not anticipate, and carrying debt with you could leave you in a dark place.

For instance, due to the housing market during one move, Carrie and I had to take a $4,000 loss on our home. An inspector found a crack in the foundation that required a major repair. We were not in a financial position to throw away $4,000, but God allowed us to find the means to make it happen. You never know.

3. **Work on your education.** It could be that you have already accomplished all the education you want, or it could be that you're continuing your education in your current ministry. If possible, finish your education sooner than later. It can quickly become a financial and even a physical burden later in life. As you take classes, stay up late, get up early, and do what you need to do. You may feel stuck where you are, but use that as a time to grow academically and spiritually. Online classes can do that, and maybe your current ministry will help you with graduate studies. But whatever you do, don't go

into debt to complete your education. Your education is important, but not that important. If possible, take some classes. It would be wonderful to have an advanced degree as you prepare for what God has for you next.

What is next is a mystery. Abraham left without even knowing where he was going. Moses would have never guessed his next step would be shepherding in the desert. Joseph would not have imagined himself in an Egyptian prison. Peter would not have guessed that he would be leaving the boats behind and fishing for men. God knows what is next.

TIME TO REFLECT
1. Where do you see yourself five years from now?
2. What are you currently doing to help prepare yourself for what is next?
3. What are some things you have been neglecting in ministry while you have been anticipating what is next?

Art of Dodging Spears

As I write this chapter, I realize it might not apply to many of you. Your church government may prevent the pastor from having rule over his assistants. In the following cases, the board rather than the pastor would be making the decisions. I give more counsel to men who find themselves in this position than any other.

When I was a kid, there was just something about having a sword in my hand that made me feel invincible. It didn't matter if it was foam or a plastic baseball bat. That sword gave me power. Coupled with my fake armor, I was unstoppable as I rode my trusty stallion (my bike) across the countryside. I was the king's hero, but more importantly the hero of his wife, Guinevere, my secret love. Many of you just took a mental journey with me back to your childhood. You know exactly what I am talking about. Today, it might not be Excalibur but your Cambridge, and it might not be the bride of King Arthur but the Bride of Christ you've been accused of stealing.

Life was awesome for Dave. He was in his third year of ministry at Fremont Church and could not have been happier. His young family was growing, and his ministry was thriving at church. People loved him, and he loved the people. He and lead pastor Matt had a great relationship as well. The pastor leaned on him for many things and continually made an effort to encourage and publicly praise the work Dave was doing.

Dave was originally hired to be an assistant to the pastor. His job description changed as the pastor's needs changed. Dave loved serving the church and especially Pastor Matt. Dave's theme verse for life and ministry was 1 Samuel 14:7, "Do all that is in thine heart: turn thee; behold, I am with thee according to thy heart."

Dave's heart and zeal were seen and experienced by everyone in the church. When guest speakers flew into town, Dave waited for them at the airport with a warm smile and pleasant greeting. When a new family visited the church, Dave knew their names, where they were from, and how many pets they owned before they walked out of the service. His only incentive was the blessing of exercising his gifts in the local church.

Dave was also a gifted teacher and communicator. Everyone enjoyed his teaching. His Sunday school class added people weekly. People were inviting people. He loved the crowd, and they loved him. Even Pastor Matt's wife started attending Dave's class because of the things she was hearing.

Dave didn't preach too many Sunday morning services, but he preached every other Sunday evening. When he began his series in the book of John, he noticed that people were taking notes on any scrap of paper they could find in their Bibles. That gave Dave an idea. He decided to put together an outline with blanks and key points from his sermon. It was a huge hit.

Dave invested in his studies, and the people responded by investing in him. They left the church singing the praises of the teaching they were receiving. They were watching this young man do something they had never seen before, and they loved it.

Despite church growth and excitement, Dave sensed that not all was good. He couldn't put his finger on it, but something was off. He wasn't sure if it was the series or the delivery style, but Pastor Matt's body language showed something different than the rest of the congregation. Tuesday morning staff meetings were also becoming very awkward when they talked about the Sunday numbers. At first, Dave took it personally, but he learned to look past it and just preach to the people he was called to serve.

Pastor Matt loved Dave, but what he saw sparked jealousy in his heart. Matt had never seen people attend or get so excited about a Sunday evening service like they were with this series in John. Jealousy gave way to bitterness and paranoia in Matt's heart. Dave was gathering a following, and he knew it was a matter of time before he would split the church or make a run to be the pastor. Matt knew he couldn't fire Dave; he was too well-loved. Besides, how do you fire a guy for bringing in crowds and teaching the Bible? Matt knew the only thing he could do was make life for Dave so difficult that Dave would quit, and that is exactly what Matt did.

Dave was doing everything he was asked to do, but he quickly found himself dodging spears. Pastor Matt was finding every little thing possible to criticize Dave. Before long, nothing Dave was doing was good enough, and he ended up running across town from Matt's presence and taking the hearts of many of the congregation with him.

What happened? Was Matt right? Did Dave do something wrong? Allow me to take the story of David and Saul (not Dave and Matt) to make some important observations.

What were the steps that led Saul to throw the spear at David?

Receiving a Thrown Spear

1. **David rejected the armor.** David, an inexperienced soldier, rejected Saul's armor, the best money could buy. Saul was willing to allow David to become another Saul. His armor was known by all. That is why Ahab gave Jehoshaphat his armor when they went into battle. Why Jehoshaphat wore it is beyond me. "And it came to pass, when the captains saw Jehoshaphat, that they said, Surely it is the king of Israel" (1 Kings 22:32). By taking the armor, everyone would have known David was sponsored and endorsed by King Saul, but David could not fight in the armor, most likely for practical reasons but philosophically because he was not endorsed by Saul but by the armies of the living God. Everything was fine until David desired to do something different.

2. **David fought with a different philosophy.** David neglected not only Saul's identity but also the traditional way of doing things. David knew exactly who he was, and God tested him multiple times to prove his strengths. God had brought him through many lion and bear-like experiences to allow him to be successful in his

current calling. David was gifted and talented in the areas he needed in order to be successful. He was a master with a slingshot, not a sword.
3. **David used wisdom.** David had become his own man. That put him in great danger with King Saul. As a hired servant and now a member of Saul's army, David was expected to do things the way everyone else always had. This was not going to work with David because that was just not who he was. He was different. He was a leader. God created him to be different, but different proved to be deadly.

Pastor Dave rejected the armor of Matt. He did things differently. Yes, it was just a 5"x11" sheet of paper, but it represented so much more. It was different. It was out-of-the-box. It was new. It was well thought out and planned. It was enhancing the preaching and teaching of God's Word, but in Matt's eyes, it was rebellion and pride.

Pastor Matt heard the praises of Dave being sung, and he could not take it. Matt's heart quickly turned from joy to jealousy. James 4 explains it best. Where there is selfish ambition and jealousy, there is every evil work. Matt's heart was producing those works rapidly.

I am afraid many of you can relate to this. Some of you bought this book and turned right to this chapter because of what you are going through. How do I know that? Because I hear it from assistants all the time. It makes me sick to my stomach, and I hurt for every one of you who has suffered through this. Just a few days ago I received a call from an assistant pastor I did not know. He was dodging spears. It broke my heart, but I had to counsel him to move on. For the sake of the church, his family, and his own well-being, he needed to transition.

I don't see this problem going away anytime soon. With the average age of an evangelical pastor increasing every year, there will be a greater age gap as time goes on. At the time of the writing of this book, the average age of the evangelical pastor is 53.8, with a median of 55. Among mainline pastors, the average was 54.8, and the median was 56. The 2020 Faith Communities Today (FACT) study of all US religious groups found an increase in the average age of clergy, climbing from 50 in 2000 to 57 in 2020. It's also interesting that the FACT report noted a correlation between the graying of the pulpit and who was sitting in the pews. The older the pastor, the heavier the concentration of senior citizens. In 2023, Lifeway published research that said pastors under age 45 lead congregations where 27 percent are 65 and older. Older pastors, on the other hand, have churches where older adults make up 40 percent of the congregation.

You might see this as bad news, but it does not have to be. Everything Dave did at Freemont was right and biblical. It really came down to a no-win situation for him. But allow me to give you a few steps to follow to possibly help prevent spears from being thrown at you.

How to Dodge a Spear

1. **Do what is asked.** "And David went out whithersoever Saul sent him and behaved himself wisely: and Saul

set him over the men of war, and he was accepted in the sight of all the people" (1 Sam. 18:5). In this text, we find David doing what Saul asked of him. If I were David, the last thing I would want to do is continue playing the harp for Saul, but he did. Granted, David's position was a little different, and the repercussions of not doing what the king asked of him could've been devastating or even life-threatening. Even in obedience, his life was still threatened, but he did what was asked of him anyway.

If you have a job description, stick to it. Or if sticking to the job description is causing friction between you and the pastor, don't be afraid to be flexible. Sometimes being right isn't worth the stress.

2. **Serve without support or applause.** In situations where spears are being thrown at you, you may need to find other ways to serve. If you are limited on how to serve your church, find ways to serve your community. Find ways to get God's Word out on social media or podcasts. If finances have been taken from you or unethically withheld, find other ways to supplement your income. You have to find ways and outlets to make the most of the situation you are in. It is easier for a pastor to put his assistant in situations where he must quit than to ask the assistant to leave. And it's much easier on the pastor's ego and less resistant if the assistant resigns. But unless God directs you to do so, you need to stay and do all you can for the glory of God in your position.

God is concerned about the church and you and the gifts, abilities, and calling He has placed on your life. You will one day have to answer God about what you are doing in your current role. If you stand before God and make excuses that the pastor wouldn't let you evangelize, preach, or visit, I don't see God being overly sympathetic.

This is exactly what Dave did. Dave had a true heart for reaching others for Christ. He knew if he brought any more people into the church, Matt would be irate. So, Dave decided he would go to the people. He made an effort to reach out instead of staying focused on what was going on within the church.

Living in Spears

The Bible says that David behaved wisely and was accepted in the sight of all the people. How should we do the same if we find ourselves in the courts of Saul?

1. **Confirm your calling.** The situation with Pastor Matt was not what Dave had signed up for. He was hired to assist the pastor, not anything else. But he knew God was in control and that he needed to make the most of the current situation. Dave knew God had placed him there. He didn't know why he was there or how long he would stay, but God wanted him in this place for this time. Sometimes, we need to take a step back from the details of our current situation and confirm our calling. Did God clearly call you here? Then, never lose sight of that reality.
2. **Love the thrower.** David would not raise his hand against King Saul. David loved Saul and his family. David never once returned the hatred Saul displayed

against him. Matt was separating himself from Dave. Their communication was beginning to be on an as-needed basis. So, one day, Dave decided he would try to change that. It was to no avail.

Matt didn't read Dave's text messages. Dave's emails were left unanswered. There was little that Dave could do to change this situation. Dave decided to give it one more go. He knew if this didn't work, nothing would. On Pastor Matt's birthday, Dave called and asked if he could take him to lunch to celebrate. Matt thanked him for this kind gesture but apologetically declined due to his busy day. Later that day, as Dave was walking across campus, he saw Pastor Matt leaving with Andy. Dave later asked the secretary where the pastor was, and she told him he was out with Andy, having lunch for his birthday. Ouch! Like David receiving the arrow from Jonathan, Dave knew he would never again be welcomed in Matt's presence. Even still, Dave had to respond lovingly to this decidedly unloving behavior. Eventually, Dave had to go, and God went with him. Dave prospered in everything he did.

TIME TO REFLECT

1. What ways can you minister to the church or community that you are not taking advantage of currently?
2. Are you handling yourself wisely in front of the people and those you serve? What are some areas where you have failed and need to adjust?
3. What is your current attitude with your senior or lead pastor? Pray, and ask God to help you love him with the love of Christ.

Art of Poverty

I want to be careful here. Money can be a touchy subject, and many views and ideas are out there. I want to share a few stories and hope to encourage you in this area if possible.

"I love having the elephant in the room conversations," said no one ever. I have been in several meetings over the years when you knew everyone there understood what the problem was, but no one had the guts to speak up. You've been there, probably countless times. It's always in the budget meeting. Staring at you is the elephant in the room, yet you sit and remain silent.

It is the night of the dreaded financial meeting with the elders. Your wife begs you to speak up this time. She sees the stress your current financial situation puts on you and is not only concerned about buying groceries but also about her husband's health. "When the subject of raises comes up," she says, "you have to let them know how much we're struggling."

Finally, the question comes. "Should we hand out raises this year?" You sit in silence. Granted, you are making the same you did five years and three kids ago, but who's counting anyway? You're thinking, *Surely the board will see everything I have done and how much help I have been around here. Without me, this ministry would be dead in a year max. They must see that.* You continue to sit in silence. "Well, I think it would be unwise to hand out raises again this year," Bill says. "I think you're right, Bill," says the pastor. "The economy is shaky; the old factory in town could close down anytime, and money doesn't grow on trees. It will be okay," he continues. "God always meets our needs."

You're thinking, *That's easy for Bill to say. It's just the two of them with a combined yearly income of more than I will make in five years.*

"But," Bill goes on to say. (Finally, Bill comes to your aid. You always liked Bill, and finally, you know he's got your back.) "Our pastor is really in need of a new car. After all, theirs is getting old, and we can't allow him to drive it much longer. Besides, what would people think if we let our senior pastor drive around in that old Chrysler?"

"I agree," says Randy from the corner of the room. "Good, it's settled then. No raises, but the car needs to be traded in before it falls apart."

The meeting is over. You have difficulty making eye contact with any of the board members as you leave. Worse yet, you know your wife is waiting at home for the big news.

If you have been in those meetings, I am sorry. I know what it feels like. The fact is that when you signed up for this (or when God signed you up), a vow of poverty seemed to come along with the calling. Somehow, many churches and senior pastors feel that having their associates live like monks or priests is good for them. It is not. Jesuit Father James Bretzke said this about living within his vow to poverty: "Poverty is also meant to mortify us."

Some of you reading this right now have been mortified. You were mortified while standing in line applying for food stamps. You were mortified while applying for WIC. You were mortified when you had to do Christmas on December 27 because you needed the Christmas bonus to be able to afford presents for your children. You are mortified every time your car pulls into a public parking lot.

But you did not take a vow of poverty. You are fully responsible for your current financial situation. Is God in control? Yes. Does God provide for your needs? Yes. Carrie and I kept a book for several years in which we wrote down all the ways God provided for our needs. But I still look back and regret allowing my family to live in poverty all those years. Because of that time, I will be continually playing catch-up for the rest of my life in regard to retirement and financial stability.

What I am going to say now is from my personal experiences. If you are looking for strategy, I recommend Dave Ramsey's financial advice for a good shot in the arm. But please remember that his book is not an appendix to the Scriptures as some make it out to be. So, what can you do now that I wish I had done when I was an associate?

Stay Away from Credit Cards

I don't care how they phrase it or how many points you earn, the credit card companies will never come out on the losing end. These are all simply ways for you to get lured into their trap. I know you can watch YouTube and read articles about people who have come away with "free" vacations, but you must understand that they already have money for vacations.

They are making the card work for them when the majority of us are working for the card. Solomon was correct when he said the borrower is the servant of the lender (Prov. 22:7). I understand that things were tight this month, so you used your card for a few purchases. But borrowing off of next month is a dangerous game. You're sure that next month will be better, and you will pay it off. Then things are even tighter next month, and before you know it, you are drowning in debt and see no way out.

Get a "Real" Job

When my oldest son was about six years old, he said out of nowhere from the back seat of the car, "Dad, I want a real job like Papaw when I grow up."

I said, "What do you mean?"

"Well, Papaw works with tools and fixes things all day. All you do is read the Bible and talk to people."

He was right. It took 10 years of living in poverty before Carrie and I finally realized I needed a "real job." The problem was I wasn't like Papaw. I can't fix anything. So, we began to pray about what we could do to help ends meet. After much prayer, we felt I needed to start a martial arts business. I love to teach, I love kids, and I love Taekwondo. I asked the pastor for permission to use the annex building on Tuesdays and Thursdays, and he graciously allowed me to do so. Long story short, we outgrew the annex gym, and I leased a building and had a very successful business.

1. **Have a Difficult Conversation.** Are you still not convinced that bi-vocational is the way to go? Then sit down with your pastor and have a heart-to-heart. Before I did this, I took my budget and income to a financial advisor (who was endorsed by Dave Ramsey) to give me some unbiased advice. After seeing my finances, he didn't even charge me for his insight. He said, "I have no idea how you can live on this." I agreed. That's why I was there. I then sat down with my pastor, told him we were struggling financially, and asked if the church could help. He said, "One time, when we were in our early years of ministry, we had no food in our house. We had no money and weren't sure what to do. When I got home from church that Sunday, someone had filled our kitchen with food. God took care of our needs. God will take care of your needs."

He was right. God's provision *was* there. But it was most likely at another ministry or second job, and I was too dumb, stubborn, and proud to consider it. You have no one to blame for your financial burden than yourself. Is your wife and family not worth providing for? Is it fair to them to be the ones without? Is poverty a sign of spirituality?

No.

Pastor, get a real job. If your church says you cannot get a second job, let them know it is fine because it will soon become your first job.

Today in America, there are many ways you can support your family. Uber, GrubHub, and grocery deliveries are things you can do in the evenings and on weekends that could put you ahead financially. Before coming here, my youth pastor was in a ministry that paid little to nothing. He and his wife shopped at yard sales and the Goodwill to find items they could resell on eBay. My current neighbor is an engineer, and he recently quit his job because he is making more money buying items from the clearance racks at major department stores and reselling them on Amazon than he ever made at his engineering firm.

Be innovative, and look for other ways to make money, and when someone asks you, "What's in your wallet?" you can say, "Cash, *not* Capital One."

TIME TO REFLECT

1. Are you being wise with your spending? What are some ways you could do better in regard to your current financial state?
2. Are you providing for your family? Is there enough in the budget to take care of their needs?
3. If you need a second source of income, what is holding you back?

Conclusion

Thank you. Thank you for fulfilling your calling as an assistant. Thank you for your desire to serve Jesus and His church. Thank you for the time, energy, and effort you have given for the ministry to continue and succeed the way that it has. Thank you for the countless hours you have worked behind the scenes with little recognition or applause. Thank you for going the extra mile for guests and visitors to ensure they have a wonderful time at church. Thank you for the sacrifices you have made. Thank you for reading this book.

As we conclude this journey through the practical aspects of being an assistant pastor, it is essential to reflect on the significant role you play in your church community. The insights and strategies shared in this book are designed to equip you with the tools necessary to navigate the unique challenges and opportunities that come with your position. Your role is multifaceted, demanding both spiritual and administrative capabilities, and it is crucial to balance your responsibilities with grace and wisdom. Reading this book was the easy part.

Now it is time for you to take the things you have read, heard, and seen in me and others and do them.

As this transpires, please never lose sight of the profound impact you have on the lives of your congregation. Your support, guidance, and presence will make a world of difference to those who are seeking spiritual growth and comfort. Remember that ministry is not merely about fulfilling duties but about fostering meaningful relationships and nurturing the faith of your congregation. By reading this book, you have already displayed a heart of compassion and dedication many pastors do not have.

Since much of this book dealt with the pastoral side, continue to strive for excellence and efficiency in your administrative duties as well. The organizational skills you bring to the table ensure that the church functions smoothly and effectively. From managing schedules to overseeing events, your ability to handle logistical details allows the senior pastor and the rest of the team to focus on their primary responsibilities. Embrace these tasks with a spirit of diligence and integrity, knowing that your efforts contribute significantly to the overall mission of the church.

Please don't forget you. Your personal growth and development are indispensable as an assistant pastor. Continue to deepen your theological knowledge, enhance your pastoral skills, and cultivate your spiritual life. Engage in regular self-reflection and seek mentorship from more experienced pastors. Your growth not only benefits you personally but also enriches your ministry and sets a positive example for others to follow.

Your role as an assistant pastor is both a privilege and a responsibility. Embrace it with humility, passion, and a heart for service. The practical tools and principles outlined in this book

Conclusion

are meant to empower you to fulfill your calling with confidence and competence. Always seek God's guidance in every aspect of your ministry, and trust that He will equip you for the tasks ahead. Your faithful service will leave a lasting impact on your church and community. It will advance the Kingdom of God and bring glory to His name.

My desire is that you will take "the things that thou hast heard of me among many witnesses, the same commit thou to faithful men, who shall be able to teach others also" (2 Tim. 2:2). Don't allow this to stop here. Find those young men in your church or community who have a desire to serve the Lord and go through this book with them.

This book may have found you on the brink of giving up or on the verge of throwing in the towel. If you are despairing even of life, I hope this book has encouraged you to continue. I trust it will inspire you to stay in the saddle and continue to "endure afflictions, do the work of an evangelist, make full proof of thy ministry" (2 Tim. 4:5).

Thank you for your dedication and commitment to serving as an assistant pastor. May you continue to grow in wisdom and grace, and may your ministry be a source of blessing and inspiration for years to come.

Milton Keynes UK
Ingram Content Group UK Ltd.
UKHW021643011224
451755UK00011B/782